Visualization

*Ultimate Workbook to Master the Game of Creative Mindfulness
Meditation Techniques and Achieve Infinite Success Through
Self Affirmation and Positive Mental Imagery*

Andrew Maltz

Published by Jason Thawne Publishing House

© Andrew Maltz

Visualization: Ultimate Workbook to Master the Game of Creative
Mindfulness Meditation Techniques and Achieve Infinite Success
Through Self Affirmation and Positive Mental Imagery

All Rights Reserved

ISBN:978-1-989749-00-5

This document is geared towards providing exact and reliable information in regards to the topic and issue covered. The publication is sold with the idea that the publisher isn't required to render accounting, officially permitted, or otherwise, qualified services. If advice is necessary, legal or even professional, a practiced individual in the profession should be ordered.

- From a Declaration of Principles which was accepted and approved equally by a Committee of the American Bar Association and a Committee of Publishers and Associations.

In no way is it legal to reproduce, duplicate, or even transmit any part of this document in either electronic means or in printed format. Recording of this publication is strictly prohibited and any storage of this document isn't allowed unless with proper written permission from the publisher. All rights reserved.

The information provided herein is stated to be truthful and consistent, in that any liability, in terms of inattention or otherwise, by any usage or abuse of any policies, processes, or directions contained within is the solitary and also utter responsibility of the recipient reader. Under no circumstances will any legal responsibility or blame be held against the publisher for any reparation, damages, or monetary loss due to the information herein, either directly or indirectly.

Respective authors own all copyrights not held by the publisher.

The information herein is offered for just informational purposes solely, and is universal as so. The presentation of the information is without contract or any type of guarantee assurance.

The trademarks that are used are without any consent, and also the publication of the trademark is without permission or backing by the trademark owner. All trademarks and brands within this book are for clarifying purposes only and are the owned by the owners themselves, not affiliated with this document.

TABLE OF CONTENTS

Chapter 1: What Is Creative Visualization?

As stated in the introduction, creative visualization is simply a mental technique guided by imagination to make your goals and dreams come true. When used in the right way, creative visualization can boost your life and take you through to the stairs of success and prosperity. It is a power that brings specific and measurable changes to your environment and influences the occurrence of certain events. To reiterate, Creative visualization can bring anything you desire from the bottom of your heart into its physical reality. This secret power in which your mind posses have the ability to achieve anything you can imagine.

If you have the ability to visualize a certain event or a particular situation, if you can hold that very thought in your mind for a long enough period of time, it has been said that you can always attract it into your life. This is much like daydreaming, to be frank, but the effects can simply be magical. Although this principle is guided by the natural ability of your mind or mental law, it can be compared to having in possession, at all times, the power of a genie in a bottle. Any wish, any thought, anything you want, at any time, can come true.

Many people use creative visualization in their day to day affairs knowingly or unknowingly. All successful people use it as a proven source of power. They simply focus on their goals and see them as already accomplished. Their focus and perseverance in this creative visualization actually brings in the success that they want in life.

Chapter 2: Role Of Visualization In Your Life

In Everyday Life

Most successful people don't get there overnight. They have to work hard every day and they change small habits about themselves in order to achieve their overall goals. You won't wake up the next morning and be the CEO of your company, or become a star football player just by thinking about it. You have to take small, measurable, actionable steps to get there.

Visualization can help you do this. Say, for instance, you want to lose weight, but you never seem to be able to get to the gym to do this. First, you have to figure out why you're not getting to the gym on time. Maybe you're running late at work because you were late for work due to not getting up on time. You've found your snag in the plan, and now you can work with it.

Visualize yourself getting up early every morning, completing your morning ritual in a timely manner, going through the workday, and finally ending up at the gym with a friend for a workout. Don't just sit by and idly watch yourself doing these things, actually taste and smell the coffee, hear the alarm clock go off, feel the water when you shower, and see what you'll be looking at throughout the day. You're training your brain to take these positive actions that will eventually lead you to getting to the gym on time.

The more you do this on a daily basis, the more it will become a reality. You'll reach your goal of losing weight in no time!

Work

Every day we do some sort of work, whether we go to a brick and mortar business, work from home or even work for ourselves. We have some sort of job to accomplish on a daily basis, and sometimes that job can be stressful. Let's use the example of an employee who must go in front of his peers and boss in order to convince them to try a new product line.

This employee has never done anything of this sort in his life and he's very nervous about the outcome. He's having some pretty dark thoughts about where this meeting might go, and finds that he's growing more and more nervous as the time approaches for him to enter the meeting room and present his idea. If this employee were to practice creative visualization, he could visualize a positive outcome for his meeting. For each negative thought, he would come up with a positive thought to counteract that one and make that positive thought more vivid in his mind.

By doing this, he would be sure to go into that meeting room with confidence and present his idea without faltering. The key to making a creative visualization work for you in a situation similar to this is to be sure to visualize everything down to the minute detail. Think about the expressions on the other people's faces, how they're sitting, what they might ask, and how you want to stand and talk. Don't forget any of the senses as they're all important in an exercise like this!

Sports

We learn through experience and observation. For example, when we learned to walk, we observed it first. We had to make that mental connection of watching someone else do it. There's a scientific phenomenon that occurs when we observe someone doing something. Our neurons transmit to one another and that mental picture is filed away, and if we really want to learn how to do what we're observing, our neurons have to break down and reconnect.

It's pretty amazing actually, but we can visualize what we want to do and our bodies will emulate what we're visualizing. You can visualize yourself taking three steps and rotating your hips to salsa music, and with some practice you'll learn how to salsa.

People who want to play a basketball game and win often visualize themselves performing the winning shot. Famous football players will take a moment before each game and visualize themselves winning. The quarterback may be visualizing how he will twist and catch the ball at the last moment and score a touchdown. The linebackers might visualize themselves tackling the other team.

You can learn the basics of a sport just by visualizing yourself succeeding.

Let's use the example of running your first marathon. Visualize how you cross the finish line in your desired amount of time and see your friends, family, or significant other waiting for you at the other end. Don't just see it, hear the sounds of cheering, see the bright colors of the tree leaves and feel the hot sun. See the time on your watch and feel the cool air over your overheated body. Process how excited you're feeling and revel in the satisfaction of knowing you did it.

Some find that it's easier to write down the goal in as much detail as possible and then imagine it. Whatever you have to do in order to get that mental image with clarity, do it.

Overall Happiness

We're unique in a way that we are mentally able to simulate situations using both the past and visualizing the future. We're also able to play a hand in creating our futures by preparing ourselves emotionally for all outcomes. This is a valuable tool that can lead us to happiness when it's applied to our goals.

Researchers have discovered that when we visualize positive or negative thoughts, we have a biochemical impact on our brains. When a psychologist asks a person to picture something they want in their life, and to create a mental image that makes this person believe their goal is achievable, they create a neurological chain of events. This chain of events changes the person's brain chemistry.

For example, I want you to imagine a beautiful beach with a warm sunset and the gentle sound of the ocean waves lapping at your feet. Feel the cool water as it touches your toes and cools you from the hot day you had sunbathing. Are you feeling relaxed yet?

Now imagine that you're at a concert and you're very close to the speakers. You can barely hear anything but the clashing of the instruments and people are pressing against you as they try to get closer to the stage. You might not be feeling as relaxed as you were a moment ago.

Visualization is a very powerful tool, and it can be used to make you feel relaxed and sure of yourself, or it can make you feel irritated and afraid.

Chapter 3: Is The Law Of Attraction

Real?

The basic answer is yes, the law of attraction is real. Whether you believe in the law of attraction or not, this law is always in effect (that is why it is called a law). Basically whatever you focus on the most, you attract more of.

The proof this law is always working is demonstrated to you in the lives of everybody around you. Look at someone you know in your life who complains a lot.

They attract plenty of things in their life to complain about their life is one big drama. Look at someone you know who is eternally upbeat. They attract plenty of things in their life to be positive about.

Even if you don't think you are consciously focusing on negative things, the fact is if you are subconsciously focusing on negative things, it is negative things you will attract into your life.

This is because our subconscious mind is much more powerful than our conscious mind. Sometimes what you want to believe is sabotaged by your subconscious mind.

At the very least, it is in your own best interests to be aware what you are focusing on. It is easy to find out where your focus lies. Take a look at your life. If it is miserable, then you are subconsciously focusing on miserable things. If your life is happy, then you are subconsciously focusing on happy things.

To turn your life around from being miserable, or to increase an already happy life you simply have to focus on more happy things. This is easier said than done because so many of our thoughts are unconscious and we are not aware of them.

Listen to your self-talk inside your head. How do you talk to yourself? Be aware how you are you internally responding to the opportunities and people in your life. With criticism or with compassion? With condemnation or acceptance? With negativity or positivity?

Think of someone you know whose life you admire and would love yours to be like. How do they live their life? See if you can copy some of their principals and adopt them into your own life.

The law of attraction is indeed a powerful force. Use it to your advantage to increase the amount of happiness and good times in your life. It does take active involvement on your part to change your subconscious thinking, but the results are definitely worth it.

Many people feel that the Law of Attraction is one of the most important things to keep in their minds as they are living their lives. This is because anything that comes to you in your life is actually something that you have attracted through the way that you think and through what your attitudes might be. Many people find that this is easy to believe when good things are happening for them.

For instance, when they've got a good job and a great partner, people tend to believe that they have attracted those things to them through positive thinking. However, when something that they feel is bad happens to them, people tend to dismiss the thoughts of positive thinking, and begin to think that the Law doesn't actually work the way that it is supposed to do.

There really is no question as to whether or not the Law of Attraction is real or not, the only question is how you are structuring your life and your attitudes so that the Law might work in your favor instead of against you. There are a few things to remember when it comes to this, so that you can be sure you are benefiting as much as you can from the Law.

First of all, the basics behind the law are very simple, and are very real. Your thoughts and attitudes are going to attract things to you. If you spend your time focusing on good thoughts, good attitudes, and good things, these will be the things that are brought to you. Likewise, if you only focus on negatives, you will end up with negative things.

The Law of Attraction is not real in only a metaphysical sense, or in a way that you have to blindly believe in. The Law is real in a concrete, for sure way. For instance, take the general idea of running late during your morning routine.

If you wake up late, and spend the rest of the morning focusing on how late you are going to be, chances are that things will happen to make you even more lately.

For instance, you might be so distraught with being late that you won't think clearly enough to remember where your shoes are, and might spill your coffee down your shirt.

However, if you wake up in the morning, even if it is late, and focus on the fact that you will still be able to make it out the door in time and don't allow any negative thoughts to enter your mind, you will be able to get back on schedule, simply by focusing your attitudes, energies, and thoughts in that manner. The Law of Attraction is indeed very real, and very important for you to remember.

The Law of Attraction revolves around training the mind to focus on your dreams and desires. You utilize your conscious and subconscious mind to tap into more of your own mental resources. These resources are already there, but most of us aren't used to using them to their full potential.

Society often sets an example based on fear. We are taught to fear not having enough money, to fear not being attractive enough and not being able to attract a partner and to fear not being good enough.

This comes from a general shame-based way of thinking which is sometimes rooted in certain religious traditions. These are very powerful forces to try to combat. They are also the reasons that using the Law of Attraction can work so well.

Using the Law of Attraction, you focus on experiencing the joy of that which you want. If you want a loving relationship, you imagine and visualize the satisfaction of feeling loved and valued.

You do not focus on the fear of being alone, but instead on your ability to experience love and all of its benefits. By feeling joy and happiness, you naturally become less afraid and begin directing your life toward your dreams and desires.

According to the Law of Attraction, you also begin to attract the things you want to you because they operate on similar frequencies which is based on actual laws of quantum physics.

I will say that I consider it unrealistic to picture yourself having a car and expecting it to materialize in your life. If, however, you go to a car dealer, test drive your dream car, and utilize the motivation generated by the feelings you have while in that car, you might be more diligent at work, inspire the boss to give you a raise, and get a little closer to having that car.

The Law of Attraction is about taking baby steps toward what you want and opening yourself up to receiving the universe's assistance. That assistance could come in two days or three months. You could also get a little today, a little more next week, and some more next month. It's all about staying open and focusing your thoughts on abundance.

Chapter 4: How Does Law Of

Attraction Work

Law of attraction is one of the most common laws of the universe that understood by most people. There are many other laws out there, but the law of attraction is one of the most famous laws of all. This is because it has been brought famous by the book, The Secret.

Many people want prosperity, love, friendship, and many things in their life. And the good news is, with the help of the law of attraction, you are able to attain any of your dreams.

The laws of attraction works based on the principle of likes attract likes. And often, it starts from your inner self, which is your mind. In other words, if you want to be rich, you must first create it in your mind. If you want to be successful in your life, think about being successful in your mind all the time.

What you need to do to make the law of attraction to work for you is to create intention and attention in your life. You have to first create the intention of getting what you want in your life. It can be money, cars, friendship, love, and happiness, anything you can ever imagine about.

After that, you will have to create the attention by focusing about the things you want in your mind and in your life. The more you focus on the things you want in your life, the more likely you are going to achieve it in your life because you are directing your life towards it.

Stop wasting your precious time, money and even your hope into the law of attraction before you finally figure out what exactly it is. It is not that the law of attraction does not work for you. It is just that you have not discover the true potential of the law and how the other laws will help you manifest what you want into your life.

As I told you earlier that "What we think, we manifest". What we are going to keep in our mind and concentrate on it, we are actually bringing it in the process of manifestation. Using law of attraction is very easy if you keep a firm belief on your thoughts and visualization. Here I will teach you how you can use the law of attraction in your life to get anything you desire to achieve. It consists of only three steps:

1. Ask

2. Feel

3. Give

Ask:

The first step is desire what you want in your life. Definitely you cannot get money if you have not planned to get it. Similarly you will not go for vacation in Spain until you have not planned it. So asking is the first step towards using law of attraction in your life. Sit down, take a pen and paper, relax and think what you desire in your life. Write down everything that comes into your mind whether it's lot of money, a good life partner or whatever... just note it on the paper. Once you have prepared the list of your dreams (wishes), proceed to the next step that is 'feel'.

Feel:

Once you have prepared a list of all of your desires, you have instructed your mind to get ready to achieve. Now start feeling like you have everything in your life that is on that piece of paper (your desires note) and already be grateful for it. If you wrote that you want a lot of money then from now onwards, start feeling like you have lot of money in your account. Bring up that joy in you when you have $100000 in your account. Feel like you have a perfect partner in your life and you are living a prosperous life. So start imagining that you have access of everything that you have written on that piece of paper and feel gratitude for this abundance. What happens here that the universe begins to listen to your these consistent thoughts and the manifestation process comes into being. So the main theme of this step is:

"What you want to achieve in your life, feel like you already have it"

Give:

The last step in the completion of the law of attraction is "to give". There is a principle in this whole process that states:

"The more you give, the more you get back"

So give from whatever you have in your life. If you can give happiness to someone, go ahead. If you have money, give it without worrying about the amount. Many people get stuck on this step and have some doubts in their minds and they are right at it. As a common person we think that dividing something reduces it. But it is opposite in the law of attraction. This law states that if you give something to someone, you shall get it back multiplied. The question is "How is it possible?" The answer is quite simple and logical. During the give process, you think like you have a lot of something say its money, and you give some money to others. This feeling of abundance ignites the second process that is 'Feel'. So when giving, feel like you already have abundance of it and you shall have abundance of it. So 'give' process helps in firming your belief that you already have abundance of everything.

This is so Easy!!

This is what law of attraction states.. Ask, feel and give. So the crux of this law lies in your thoughts. Negative thoughts will bring up negative circumstances and vice versa. So start using the law of attraction in your life from now onwards. In the beginning it will take some time to control your thoughts and keep them positive but gradually you will start to have grip over your thoughts and things will start working as the law of attraction will come into action. Its you who can change your life right now and forever. So go ahead and take advantage of this law and be happy. Good luck.

Chapter 5: Visualization Techniques

Visualization techniques fire up our minds to use its untapped potential to succeed and reach goals. Visualization is merely a process of mental imagery where we picture ourselves experiencing the things that we truly desire. Our imagination is the largest factor because it is the ONLY thing that we need for the entire process. Imagination is, indeed, greater than knowledge.

Knowledge has limits. Imagination is limitless. Imagination enables us to design the life that we want to live, along with all other experiences associated with it. It lifts our spirits up by making us feel good while we think of what we desire. Little did we know that our innocent-looking imaginations could be the answer to all our problems, and reaching the tip of the mountain! Now that you know that imagination is your limit, how far do you think you can go?

World-class athletes use visualization techniques to become successful in their respective sports. A scientific investigation conducted on four athlete groups has proven that those who have excellent visualization skills are more likely to be winners than those with only physical training. It can be undeniably concluded that the experiences in our subconscious minds are the same as the actual events in the outside world.

Treasure Draw

Treasure drawing means making a picture of something that we desire. We usually draw it if it's possible to draw. We place it wherever we can easily see it every day (e.g. on the kitchen wall, your bedroom ceiling, the fridge door). Treasure drawing provides you with a clear picture of what you really want to accomplish, thus helping you bring your goals to life.

Reformed Memory Visualization

A technique called reformed memory visualization is used in resolving conflicts and setting aside angers of the past. With this technique, you are putting graphical scenarios in your mind where you deliberately replace negative elements with positive ones, specifically the emotion you put into it. In a basic sense, it alters the negative past to produce a positive future. This provides great assistance to people who have experienced something bad in the past. For instance, in lieu of mourning tragedies or blaming someone, you tend to transform that emotion, thinking that it serves a great purpose for your life. Once you recall the scene, try not to become angry and remain calm by breathing placidly. It will take time to recreate the same scenes over and over again, but you'll get there eventually.

Open Visualization

Watching a movie in your mind, with you as the director, is called the open visualization technique wherein you have all the power to control that particular movie. A solemn, receptive place is good for an exercise where a student can visualize the outlook of a unique pictorial experience. Undergoing this activity is best accompanied with music.

Directed Visualization

Directed visualization is described as the method of choosing the scenery in your mind and feeling it as if it were real. People use this f visualization technique to find a spot inside them where there is great connection to their intuition. People using this type of visualization form solutions using the scenes they've visualized. By conceiving imagery, their conscious minds bring up questions as well as answers.

Examples

For someone who is confused in his way, visualization could put him on the right track. You can participate in visualization seminars wherein you get to listen to a speaker who can help you achieve more through visualization, in addition to the great help this book has already given you. Furthermore, speakers can get your heat turned up as they can speak graciously and with energy. Individual sessions are also available for people who want to have a more personal approach in practicing visualization. Having a private session could also satisfy your individual needs. Spending some time with this inner journey is also good for your health. Sooner or later you will start feeling better, and you'll notice more signs of positive changes. Educating yourself with visualization techniques will pave the way to revitalizing both your mind and spirit, thus training yourself will make attracting the things you want easier. With sufficient self-control and intuition, you put yourself on track for the things that you deserve.

To get more from treasure draw, you can do things to help intensify your visualization other than clarifying your goals and the corresponding milestones along the way. Note that you are not entirely obligated to literally draw the things that you want. You can also cut pictures from magazines, such as a nice house, a brand new car, or any picture that depicts something that you want. If magazines are not available, you can always search for images in the Internet and print them. The next thing you have to do is paste them on a visualization board. This is just a simple cardboard box or illustration board with the collage of everything that you want on it. The last step is to paste it on the wall where you can see it every day.

Note that visualization and imagination are fundamentally the same in approach. To visualize something is to simply imagine it. The human mind is so magnificent that it can see and understand information that a picture delivers in addition to functioning cognitively. The subconscious mind has its own behavioral reaction and emotional response to every image it has seen. At first, you can't visualize vivid pictures but, with patience and practice, you can become better as you strive. You don't need to be an expert in visualizing things, but you have to be good enough on your own.

Chapter 6: More On Visualization Techniques

There are many ways to visualize the changes you envision for your life and their effects. It could be an audio or video inspiration, a friend who guides you through your visualization or a quick mental flash you get that gives you inspiration or a surge of energy and motivation towards your dreams. All these types of visualizations are grouped into three main techniques. It is important to understand these categories. They can help you know how and when to use them. It is also the best way to ensure any affirmations used to encourage yourself achieve the results you want in your life.

1.   Unguided Visualization

This is the kind of visualization you practice unconsciously. Usually, you find yourself following the flow of your thoughts without making great effort to control them. It is an instant visualization where you become a detached observer like in a dream. It could be a story you imagine as you read it, a vista you visualize as you listen to music, or you could be dreaming and daydreaming. These are all unguided visualization.

It is the flashes of inspiration when an idea or picture suddenly pops into your mind; the "aha" moments when things simply become clear and make sense or you suddenly get a solution to whatever problem you have or get an epiphany. It may be impossible to control these flashes. Furthermore, you can have them happen all day without realizing it.

a) Daydreaming

Daydreaming is more like dreaming in your sleep only that you are awake in a dream-like state. It is a natural mechanism that happens mostly when you are bored or tired. Your sight becomes blurred as you gaze into the distance and all the distractions are removed from your line of vision. Since you are awake, many of the daydreams you get will be of things important to you at that time. Although it is possible to have some form of control on this kind of visualization, your thoughts will still be all over the place.

It is an important type of visualization. It is a reflection you can use to order your thoughts and to understand them better. It can also be a good way for you to rebuild the neutral pathways in your brain. This is where the neutron in your brain reprograms itself by creating new connections and strengthening existing ones to make you learn more. Using daydreams it becomes easy to analyze life in a deeper and detached manner that can easily make it possible to cope with life. You can use it to sort out any changes you experience in your life.

b) Lucid dreaming

This happens when you are asleep. In a
dream state, you can actually take control
of the happenings in your dream when
your conscious mind "wakes up" in the
dream. Here, you become a participant
and less of an observer. Your sleep dream
is often guided by the unconscious mind.
This means you have no control over it and
have no way of choosing which dreams to
have or not to have, good or bad. That is
why you always find yourself in scenarios
that you would never even think of when
you are daydreaming. It is also the reason
you have nightmares.

Your unconscious mind can use your
dream to pass a message to you. Often,
dreams arise due to your fears, worries or
concerns. Therefore, if you have more
nightmares it could mean that is an issue
in your life that needs to be addressed.
You can use lucid dreaming to make sense
of your day. It can also serve as a way to

lay down all the memories important to you. This is all done in an abstract way.

It is impossible to change whatever is happening in a lucid dream. This is because your unconscious mind is driving your dreams for you. However, in a dream it is easy to look closely at objects, study the finer details and notice the subtlest of things. Life in a lucid dream all appears in three dimensions and very much clearer than real life is. There is no one way to explain a lucid dream. Often times, you will have trouble believing your dreams. However, the experience is sensational.

How can you take advantage of lucid dream? It is possible to wake your conscious mind in a dream and transform your normal dream into a lucid dream. First, try to explore the world presented in your dream. You should touch and feel things and even try the imaginable like flying. Secondly, once your conscious mind becomes awake you can incorporate your visualizations into your dream. Here, you can imagine yourself doing the things you want to do to improve your life or the changes you desire in your life. You can even act your goals out, exaggerate them and make them real.

Turning a dream into a lucid dream

First, you should know that lucid dreaming can easily take place if you have gone long periods without sleep. It can also happen when you take a nap after a main sleep, or during nap time in the middle of the day. This sleep is usually lighter. This makes it easy for your conscious mind to take control and enable you create a lucid dream. As you take your nap, recognize that lucid dreaming is possible in this state. This makes it possible for you to recognize and take advantage of it.

Secondly, you can use creative visualization to create a lucid dream. The idea here is to visualize yourself asleep, "waking up" into a lucid dream and imagining what you would do when you are in that state. This is a way to let the unconscious mind know you want a lucid dream.

Thirdly, you can also bring on lucid dreams and continue to experience it if you keep the concept foremost in your thought. There is a lot of information online and books you can read about how to create lucid dreams.

Visualizing at the spur of a moment

It is not a must you set aside time to experience sensational visualization. You only need to get yourself relaxed and create the right mood for visualizing. You can fall asleep if this will help.

Reinforcing visualization

This kind of visualization allows you to build on existing situations or skills. Your unconscious mind will focus on those things you visualize on. You can visualize reinforcing feelings of strength, endurance, will power or a habit you think is right for your life. This visualization can be both negative and positive. However, you get better results if you concentrate on positive visualizations.

Interrupt visualization

You can easily replace unwanted patterns in your life using interrupt visualization. This is where you interrupt a course of action that would normally lead to undesired ending. Usually, you stop yourself at that point before the harmful ending by making something else happen by focusing on something else.

As you get accustomed to unguided visualization, opportunities present themselves where you can make quick visualization. You should take advantage of them to help you make sense of your current situation or life. New visualization reinforces the one before and this will help you take the right steps towards achieving any goal you have in your life.

2.   Guided Visualization

If you consciously take control of your visualization and provide a course for it from start to end this is a guided visualization. Here, you take an active control to visualize constructively. It is also a process where you structure how you think and your visuals to help you discover or develop new skills. The idea is to visualize yourself doing the things you want and how you feel when you do them. This is the kind of visualization that can help you shape how your future pans out.

It is the mirror neutron in your brain which is used to make connections when you observe actions by others to make you feel

38

like you are the one carrying out the action. You have to imagine yourself doing the same thing at the moment to feel the inspiration. Furthermore, you are more likely to remember the things you see in your visualization if you take in more information about it. During this process, the neurons in the brain connect to help you learn the new skill.

Following a Visualization Plan

You need a plan if your guided visualization is to work. It is this plan that works to help you complete each visualization process you start. It could be an existing plan you get from a book or various resources or you could design your own guide. Make sure your plan has a beginning, middle and an end. When using your plan, make sure you do not lapse back to unguided visualizing.

a)   Audio and Video Assistance

These visualization guides work best when you are starting your visualization process. It is also the ideal way to start visualizing if you find it hard to use your imagination in the initial stages of the process. They come as CDs and websites with videos that narrate and guide you on how to visualize on your own. The narrations touch on specific issues and goals. As you become skilled in visualizing the more you rely less on the audio and video assistance.

b)   Guide from a Friend or Relative

There are people who already understand creative visualization. If you know a friend or family member skilled in visualizing you can ask them to help you in the exercise. Have them describe the process and let yourself imagine them in your mind. Do not despair if you do not know anyone who can do it. You can have a friend read a visualizing guide for you as you visualize. You can also read the visualization resources from your computer or a recording device and play it back as you visualize. The best visualization process requires your whole attention. Therefore, having a friend read for you or recording yourself lets you commit the exercise into your memory. It also helps to memorize one or two exercises and try to recall them when you need to visualize.

c)   Mental Flash Cards

It is possible to get small flashes of visualization within the main visualization at the same time. To do this you can create a quick summary of a longer visualization and use this short version when you do not have time to practice a longer visualization. This is a great exercise you can use when faced with a situation that requires you to make quick decisions.

d)   Write down Your Visualization

At the beginning of a visualization process it may be difficult to use your imagination, by writing down your visualization you can return to them later. This is also a good way to enhance you visualization process and reinforce a goal you have in mind. Since the goals are written down, you cannot change them.

You need to set yourself goals and write them down on a piece of paper with a deadline for achieving them. For more effectiveness you need to sign and date the piece of paper. Pin the written visualization to a wall or a strategic place like the bathroom mirror where you can easily reach or see. Let this be a constant reminder to spur you into frequent visualization. Once you achieve these goals you should modify them or replace them with new goals.

Chapter 7: Good Vibrations Make The

Law Of Magnetism Happen

You're only as good as the things you have in your head.

Here's the thing about life: when you make use of positive thoughts, you get to help yourself feel better. You get to help yourself realize that you're not just the person you are now, but that you can be the kind of person that you have always wanted to become. And with that, you'd get to manifest abundance in your life.

As a person, you get to place certain frequencies on yourself. According to scientists, there are strings of energy in the universe, and these strings are the positive and negative vibrations in life. The more you think negatively, the more negative vibrations you get to have in your life. On the other hand, when you make use of positive thinking, you get to attract positive vibes in your life. Manifesting power becomes easy. You'd get to feel like you're actually worthy of having a wonderful life.

Success in an Imperfect Life

So, maybe, you're thinking: I don't even have a perfect life. I have all these things I have to deal with. How can I feel better, then?

And you know what? It's true. Life is not perfect. In fact, life is not actually fair for most people. There are people who go through things that their peers have not experienced before. That's enough to make you feel like you deserve better in life, and you know what? You do. You deserve better in life, and it has to start with you.

You see, if you focus too much on the negative things in life, you really won't feel better about yourself, and you'd just be in this state of self-pity—which will only take minutes and hours of your time, and make you feel like you are not worthy of anything.

Focus on Your Strengths and Learn to Motivate Yourself

What can you do then? Well, first, you should be able to focus on your strengths first. By knowing what your strengths are, you easily get to know which fields you'll excel in, and you would realize that you can actually do a lot of amazing things. Here are some questions that you could answer:

• What is one thing that you do that you know you do better than anyone else?

• How do you think you're able to influence people?

• What do most people see as your strengths?

• What are the advantages in life that you know you have?

• What connections do you have?

• Which personal resources do you have access to?

By answering these questions, you get to analyze yourself more—and understand what you need to do to reach your goals. Afterwards, you have to learn how to motivate yourself. You see, in life, no one would really motivate you unless you try to do so yourself. Waiting for someone to motivate you would just make you waste a whole lot of time.

Therefore, you have to make sure that you have a clear mind, and to do that, you have to motivate yourself. When you do that, you can focus on what you have to do, and make the best decisions for your life!

For this, you can do the following:

Pre-commit when you know you're going to procrastinate. This means that you should remind yourself that you are already committed to something, because with that thought in mind, you could push yourself not to procrastinate.

Make use of a vision board. Put it where you'd always see it to remind yourself of where you're going. Add quotes that you know will motivate you.

Know that others are relying on you. In this world, no man is an island. Whatever it is that you're doing in life is significant to others' lives, too.

Create Momentum. Instead of saying you're going to get $10,000 in a month, think about what you can do each day to get there first. Think about what you can make it a week first. There is nothing wrong with starting small.

Remember that for everything you finish, you get a chance to move on to the next level of success. This is so much better than getting stuck where you are!

Chapter 8: Thinking Faster

If you are slow with your answers and unable to find solutions quickly, visualization helps with this as well. Sluggish minds are like that because they are too busy trying to solve problems that cannot be solved. In the example of the mother and her child, she filled her mind with blame and resentment. She wasn't able to see beyond that because she was, in effect, grieving the loss of the relationship. Of course, there are times that people need to do that although it's healthier to think happy thoughts because this helps to take away resentment and encourage abundance in your life. This also helps you to get over problems and things you cannot change. She was unable to think fast because her mind was too filled with blame.

Now take a look at the things that you think about. Logically speaking, if you are busy with one job, you can't do another very well at all. Visualization helps you because instead of thinking about how long the washing machine will take or what time visitors are coming, you simply visualize happy things. The washing machine will finish when it finishes regardless of what your thoughts are. The visitors will arrive when they arrive, and there's not much you can do about that. People fill their minds with unnecessary detail. When they do that, they cannot give quick responses because their minds are too occupied.

Exercise:

Sit in a comfortable chair. Focus on something across the room. Do not be distracted by anything such as TV or noise, pets or kids. Make sure you do this all on your own. Stay focused. Breathe in and concentrate on the breath. Feel it filling your lungs. Then, breathe out through your mouth but make sure that you breathe out more air than you breathe in. Concentrate on the breathing. Do not think of anything. Try this for five minutes. Then get someone to test you for responses. You will find that you will be able to answer questions very quickly because what you just did was relax your mind. What you visualized was your breathing. This is almost like a form of meditation and sharpens the mind. In this instance, you will find that you can give quick responses. If you are going to have a meeting at work and are worried about giving responses, take five minutes out of your day beforehand and use the meditation visualization to get you ready to take on the questions which may come out of that meeting. You will be sharp and ready to answer any questions which are asked.

The same tactics can be used before important events at any time during your life. You are visualizing your breathing and nothing else and in doing so, oxygenate your body and allow your brain to function in a quicker way.

Practice it and you will find this really does help you to think quicker when you need to be able to. This lets your mind work out answers and process information much quicker than it normally would.

Get someone to test you. Use it for examination questions and you will be passing exams like a pro. It's just a case of making your mind do your work for you, using visualization. When you are learning, your mind is absorbing information provided that the mind is receptive to this information. What stops it quite frequently is having too much already filling your mind. Getting used to using visualization you can become more creative. You can also get through exams without having to worry about them. Often, if you approach exams with a negative mind, you will fail. If you approach them with happy and contented thoughts after a moment of quiet breathing meditation, you are much more likely to get great grades.

The difference is always the approach to the next moment. Visualize happy things, and happy results come as a consequence. Visualize bad things and as a consequence of these thoughts, the natural result is that you will fail. Visualization is that powerful. Try it and see. All you have to waste in trying is one moment of your life. That moment will dictate how you approach the next moment of your life.

Chapter 9: Principles Of The Law Of Attraction

When Rhonda Bryne released not just the book but followed it up with the movie The Secret back in 2007 there was a lot of media acclaim and hype on the subject. However, in as much as a lot of people were keen on addressing this issue, what came out clearly was the fact that this was not the first time that such was coming to pass. There has been a lot of talk about the power of the Law of Attraction in the past, with writers like Jerry and Esther Hicks, the Late Lynn Grabhorn and Michael Losier also weighing in on the topic in different capacities and through their different literary works.

Despite all the criticism that has been leveled against this law by critics and other fascists one thing that we can be sure of is that the Law of Attraction does work in real life. Indeed like any other law out there or rule of law, it takes a lot of hard work and determination to make things work besides just willing it in your mind. When you follow and adhere to the principles that guide this law, you will most certainly be one of those success stories we will see running on Oprah and other media channels that have been at the helm of showcasing the reality behind the Law of Attraction, and the power that the human mind possesses, if only we channel our energy in the right way.

The following are the basic principles of the Law of Attraction that you would be best placed to learn about:

Sympathetic vibrations

Everything that makes up the universe often vibrates in relation to one another. When you put two things together and you strike one of them, the other will most certainly have a reaction more or less similar to the one before it. Human beings often vibrate feelings which in most case are amplified by the things that the things that we think about. It is on this premise that the Law of Attraction underlines the concept that like attracts like.

As a result, when you start thinking about something good or bad, your body will vibrate the sensation and the feelings to the point where you will find yourself coming to live in the reality of your thought process.

Raising the vibrations

There can only ever be two feelings that we encounter from time to time; either good or bad. The Law of Attraction proposes that you should learn to raise your vibrations; learn to appreciate the importance of feeling good about yourself.

Let's take a simple example; on a day when you wake up in a really bad mood, have you ever noticed how everything seems to go so wrong in the day? You end up feeling like the whole world is conspiring against you, trying to make you look or feel even worse than you already do. However, when you have a good morning, it seems like everyone else is in a good mood, everyone else is trying to make sure that you keep that mood going along.

According to this law, the things that you feel are resonated through the day, through your thoughts and emotions. It is therefore important that you learn to know your body well enough, and to make sure that whenever something happens to you, you can learn to tell the positivity or the negativity that comes with it, and combat it in the best way possible.

Mood changes are within your power

Believe it or not, there is only ever one person that can change your moods — yourself! To be honest, no one can claim that they always wake up feeling good about themselves, or that they never have bad experiences. Bad encounters are just a way of life, something that happens to the best of us all. However, just because you are having a bad day does not necessarily mean that you should keep the rest of the day feeling sour. You have the power to change your moods by thinking straight, by thinking about all the good things and most importantly changing the way you perceive of things. Remember that every good deed or thought that you make in your day will keep resonating and before you know it, you have yourself one amazing day.

The process to deliberate creation

There is a four step process towards feeling good about yourself and feeling good about everything that exists around you. We may have mentioned earlier on how important it is to make sure that you find the balance in the universe and use it to your advantage. The following steps should help you live through this principle:

Identify what you want and what you do not want

Be clear about the same; what you want and what you do not want

Feel good about having the things you want

Open up to the universe to get you the things you desire

These simple sub-principles might sound so easy, but rest assured that there is so much more to it than meets the eye. As a matter of fact, once you can follow this process step by step, you will be able to enjoy everything this law has to offer.

Remove all doubt

Of all the principles, this final statement could perhaps be one of the most important. The absence of doubt means so much to you especially when you want to achieve your goals. the presence of doubt only works towards wasting your time, and delaying the success process that the Law of Attraction could have in as far as your goals are concerned.

Generally these principles could be very easy for some people to follow, while for some it could be quite the daunting task. However, rest assured that success only comes to those who will it. As a result of this you have to pay attention to detail, especially to the things that happen in your life, learn the positives and the negatives, and most importantly how to turn your situations around and make

things work in your favor. By the end of
the day, all the power is in your mind.

Chapter 10: Deciding What To Manifest

The statement, "You can do anything you put your mind to," leads us to think that all you have to do is imagine what you'd like to achieve, set your mind to the task, and await success.

To a certain degree, this is true. Focused intention blended with action is a potent force. However the statement is misleading as it fails to mention the difficulty and necessity of focusing your mind on a particular goal.

What Do You Want

Most of us do not know what we wish. We believe we do, however we truly do not. We only know what we do not wish. We do not wish an awful job. We do not wish to be destitute. We do not wish to disappoint our family.

Knowing specifically what you wish is much different than recognizing what you do not wish. When you solely know what you do not wish, your intentions aren't focused and you manifest the bad. Consider this illustration.

Bill doesn't wish to be destitute. He's sick of bringing in less than his friends, and he's determined to advance his status. To achieve this goal, Bill could take a lot of different paths. He could train for a high paying job, like doctor or lawyer. He might begin his own company, go into real estate, or do a lot of other things that would lead to bringing in wealth.

However Bill isn't sure what he wants to do. He doesn't understand which path best fits his skills and personality, so he doesn't resolve to follow any certain path.

Hoping to answer this question, he investigates many possibilities, however as soon as he runs into hardship he decides that path isn't for him and moves on to a fresh solution.

Bill's actions aren't focused. Although he works really hard, his efforts do not build on one another. Instead of building one giant impenetrable sand castle, Bill has established 20 little ones that are easily toppled. He winds up confused and disheartened. Finally Bill's lack of focus leads to failure.

Now, what if Bill had selected a particular path, particular goals to manifest? Suppose he chose on the law profession. His actions and things to manifest would have been clearly defined:

- Get an elevated score on the LSAT
- Get letters of recommendation
- Become accepted at a great law school
- Choose a field of law
- Gain a law degree
- Find a high paying job with a great law firm

A set of particular goals is much simpler to accomplish and to manifest than a vague end goal like getting rich. Being focused on a path gives Bill a logical set of actions to manifest. Each achievement is one step closer to the final goal.

I think we may all agree that committing to a distinctly defined path for manifesting, regardless of which one, gives Bill the greatest chance of getting to be wealthy.

However how may he select a path if he doesn't know what he wants? Perhaps cash isn't his only goal. Perhaps he wishes to do something he loves at the same time. Perhaps he can't afford to go back to school. Realism is complicated, and Bill doesn't wish to commit too soon.

And that's why he fails.

However I do not think that's inevitably a bad thing. Most individuals do not fit neatly into a predefined path. Forcing yourself into one might lead to success; however it likely won't make you happy.

This is the point. If you wish to be conventionally successful, to attain riches and status, you have to choose a particular path (preferably something mainstream) and work at manifesting each step.

On the other hand, if you aren't especially concerned with riches or success, you may take your time searching for that perfect life.

Just do not wait too long to choose. Every moment you deliberate, is a moment you lose.

Chapter 11: Float Away Visualization

Allow your body to relax. Your arms and hands can rest on your sides or on your heart chakra folded, or on your knees. Make sure you're wearing clothes that are comfortable and not too tight.

Close your eyes and allow yourself to feel the experience. Try to silence your mind without any thoughts. If you have any just let them come in and roll away like waves that gently approach the lakeshore.

Waves slowly come in and go back out one by one. Every thought should roll with the tides. Every emotion should roll forward and backward, inward and outward.

Give yourself time to just enjoy the relaxation for a few minutes. You are free to be in your own space and time. You have nowhere to be at this particular moment in time. There is nothing you have to do at this particular moment in time.

Your mind might drift off into different thoughts, but bring your focus back to the present experience.

Breathe in deeply. Breathe in positive energy. Breathe in love energy. Exhale the negative energy and exhale the anger energy. Do this three to five times in a row.

Feel yourself in a warm gentle place. You are now in a safe place where no one can ever harm or hurt you. A place that is your very own unique place and no one can access this place, but you.

Let go of any ideas of what you should experience or not experience. Allow yourself to be you. Allow the experience to flow naturally. Breathe at your own pace and what is comfortable for you.

Imagine yourself on a heart shaped beach. The only emotions and feelings you can experience is love. Love is all you know. Breathe in pure love.

The sapphire sky is painted with white puffy clouds that float one by one. They are so soft and plush. The clouds look warm and cozy as you look up into the sky. Watch the clouds shape into a heart of love.

Aqua waves are calm and still. The water is crystal clear and you can see to the bottom of the ocean. You step into the warm water and feel the sun caress your rosy cheeks. The water feels relaxing and refreshing to your skin.

You sink beneath the warm crystal clear surface and rest your head. You float away as the water holds you softly and cradles you with love.

You can hear the sounds of seagulls fly above. You can see them spreading their small wings as they glide across the sapphire skyline. You feel peaceful as you sit back and enjoy the experience.

You see two white swans nearby. Slowly you swim towards them.

Experience each stroke as you swim closer and closer to them.

You stand five yards from the swans. Notice how pure and white the swans seem.

Notice how beautiful they move together across the lake together in unison. You rise out of the warm water on to the lakeshore and sit and watch them follow you under the bright sun.

Pick up one of the swans soft feathers off the ground. Feel the stem of the feather and all the little tiny slivers that shape it. Tickle your face with the tip of it. Feel the smile on your face brighten.

Smiling feels wonderful. You can feel the love glow in your heart. You can feel the warmth of being blessed by love.

The swans remind you how nice it is to live in unity and harmony with nature. Feel the brilliant sunshine warm your body.

Allow yourself to fill up with as much love as possible. Allow love to radiate through your whole being. Allow it to magnify the positive aspects of yourself. Remember love is a beautiful experience.

Hold this feeling as long you would like. When you're ready to end this meditation you may at any time.

Just open your eyes. Relax for a few minutes and allow yourself to reflect over the meditation and allow your body to adjust back to normal.

Chapter 12: How Mindfulness Can Quiet Your Roving Mind

To be truly creative and productive, you must find a way to focus your mind and energy. Once you are focused, you will be able to work more efficiently, avoid all kinds of distractions, and make the most out of your time. Focus and clarity also help increase the brain's performance and stimulate creativity for the whole day.

Meditation: The Key to Achieving Focus

Focus is just one of the many benefits of learning to meditate. Meditation helps increase mindfulness, cleanses your mind of distractions and doubts, teaches your body to relax and breathe properly, and also promotes positive mental health. Below is simple guide to help you perform a breathing meditation ritual.

1. Look for a quiet, clear place.

Experts in meditation like monks and priests can usually meditate even if they are in the midst of a crowd or a busy place.

However, for beginners, the amount of distractions around them might hinder them from gaining true insight and peace of mind. To avoid this, you must search for a quiet, clear place where you can relax.

You can meditate in your room, in your living room, or even in your office, as long as you are able to stop yourself from being distracted. It would help if the place you meditated in is clean, with as little objects or furniture in the way.

2. Sit properly.

Once you have found a suitable place to meditate, you must learn how to sit properly for the meditation ritual. Sit cross-legged on a meditation or yoga mat. The surface you choose to sit on must be flat and even. Straighten your back, and sit in such a way that you can breathe easily and slowly. Bring your hands together, but do not grip each hand so tightly. Place your hands at the center of your legs, or hold them under your ribs.

3. Breathe in and out slowly.

Breathe naturally. Pay close attention to how you breathe. Is it too fast? Too slow? Are other things weighing on your mind? If so, make an effort to forget them for the time being. Teach yourself to focus on what you are already doing.

Concentrate on your breathing. Inhale and exhale gently. At first, your mind will undoubtedly be crowded with worries and stress. Do not let them get the better of you. Acknowledge that your worries exist, and then push them away from your mind. Rest reassured that you will be able to solve your problems and complete your tasks later. For now, you have to mind your breathing and clear your head.

Continue breathing in and out at a natural pace until you are no longer thinking of anything else. You will know that your mind has cleared because you will feel your body start to relax, and you will be filled with a quiet kind of confidence, an assurance that stems from within yourself.

Slowly open your eyes. Take one last deep, calming breath.

You are focused. You are ready to take on the day and whatever challenges it may bring. You are ready to be creative and productive.

Chapter 13: Innovations In Creative Renewal

Whether your idea of renewal is upcycling, making something old new again, or something completely different, there is no doubt that renewal of any kind takes innovation and creativity. The stories in this chapter will no doubt warm your heart and perhaps inspire you in a little creative renewal of your own.

Roger Norris Gordon, CoFounder and President of Food Cowboy

Forty-three billion pounds of food rot in garbage dumps each year because it gets bruised or damaged on the way to local grocers. If you consider world hunger rates, this is ludicrous. Roger wasn't willing to let it happen. Of course the delivery of this food to those in need is too expensive an endeavor for the companies shipping the produce.

What did Roger do? He jumped on his computer and helped his brother and many other truck drivers find a home for their unwanted loads at shelters close to the truckers' locations. Then he started thinking about Mobile technology and how most, if not all, trucks have smart phones. This could make the ease of finding a location for their damaged, but still edible haul as simple as sending a text message.

In 2012, Food Cowboy was born. Roger and his brother founded the company which is essentially a web application that allows truckers to be matched to local shelters where they can drop unwanted food. The food gets into needy hands and is kept out of the garbage dump. Hundreds of truckers have signed up. Together they have saved more than 500,000 pounds of food. This has garnered attention from the U.S. Department of Agriculture who hopes an expo on the subject will bring more ideas like Roger's.

Roger recognized a need and filled it with a waste. In so doing, though, he stopped a shameful waste of life-giving food.

Michael Phillips Moskowitz, Chief Curator at eBay

In 1995, eBay was founded in a San Jose living room. Since then, it has been an Internet staple. You would probably be hard-pressed to find an avid Internet user who doesn't have a log in for this giant online yard sale. Since its inception, it has grown and evolved over the years, but managed to maintain the model with which it began.

Secondhand shoppers are no longer limited to local shops. They can shop the world for treasures among another person's unwanted items.

So, what could be better? Michael found a way to highlight the coolest items he and his team found through the medium of curation. Content curation is just a fancy term for organizing content in a list or under a specific theme and presenting it in a meaningful way. Anyone with an eBay log in can access Michael and his team's collections like "Retro Redux" or "The Natural World".

Michael's collections are more than just lists. Michael focuses on the story and retells that story as a part of every collection he puts together. It's the story that sells the items and brings millions of users looking for his lists. He creates a meaningful experience to accompany each item he curates and that's what sells merchandise.

Michael's recognition that the story is just as important as the items connects with an audience who feels the same way. This personal connection makes Michael's creative renewal innovation a success!

(Sources:
http://www.cs.brandeis.edu/~magnus/ief 248a/eBay/history.html

http://www.bethkanter.org/content-curation-101/)

Billy Parish, CoFounder and President of Mosaic

When it comes to fossil fuels and clean energy, there is a lot of controversy. As people, we recognized long ago that we needed to let go of fossil fuels and move on to cleaner, renewable energy sources. This transition has yet to happen; however, with advocates like Billy Parish, we will begin to see such changes happen more quickly.

Billy is fully aware that the reason our transition to clean energy is so slow is because fossil fuels generate a staggering amount of revenue for fuel companies. When he launched Mosaic in 2013, he asserted that "The shift from fossil fuels to clean energy represents one of the largest wealth-creation opportunities of our time, if we can democratize ownership of the assets."

That's exactly what Billy sought to do with Mosaic. It's actually a crowd-funding platform that connects investors with solar projects that are under-financed. Anyone who has as little as $25 to spend, can invest. This has produced $7 million for commercial projects, but Billy hasn't stopped there. In early 2014, Mosaic began funding loans for residences too.

Billy broke down our hesitation, found a solution, and moved forward to innovate in the much-needed area of renewable energy. The Earth will thank him one day.

Theaster Gates, Artist, Founder of Rebuild Project, and the Director of Arts and Public Life at the University of Chicago

What do you get when you mix art with a taste for good culture? The answer is Theaster Gates. Theaster started at a residential level on the South Side of Chicago when he needed a place to live in 2006. He has transformed empty homes into cultural spaces. He also turned a former housing project into residences and a hub for the arts.

Theaster's latest project is the transformation of an old bank building into a library that will house an archive of African-American history. In addition, it will also include a restaurant. This will provide for a significant need on the South and West sides for a place to get a drink and a nice meal.

At the same time, Theaster is also tackling a giant art project for the Chicago Transit Authority. Rather than lock into a specific theme for the project, Theaster has partnered with area radio stations to create content to inspire residents to think outside the box about what kind of art this project should include. Theaster concludes that by doing so, he will foster artistic leadership rather just artistic production.

Theaster has sought to include culture in the public space in a big way because he knows that culture should be central to how the human landscape functions.

Chapter 14: The Conscious And The Subconscious

The Conscious Mind

The conscious mind is the part of your mind that is responsible for logic and reasoning. If I asked you to multiply two times six, it would be your conscious mind that would make the calculation and arrive at twelve.

The conscious mind also controls every action that you do intentionally while being conscious. If you decide to take a sip of your tea or coffee and lift the cup to your mouth, that is done by your conscious mind. Anytime you're aware of something you're doing you can be sure that you are doing it because of your conscious mind.

The conscious mind is also known as the gate keeper of the mind. You could also think of it a filter that allows some some good and some bad things to come through. You have the power to control what comes through and this will be discussed later on.

If someone tried to present you with a belief that doesn't match your belief system then your conscious mind will filter that belief. If someone were to tell you that the sky is orange, your conscious mind would instantly filter or reference your lifetime of experience and knowledge that tells you that this statement isn't true. This statement, "The sky is orange", wouldn't make it through the gate.

Subconscious Mind

The subconscious mind is the part of your mind responsible for all of your involuntary actions. Your breathing, heartbeat, digestion and all involuntary bodily functions are controlled by your subconscious mind.

If you started to control your breathing rate by intentionally increasing or decreasing it, your conscious mind would be in charge while if you were just breathing normally without trying to control the rate, your subconscious mind would be in charge.

Your emotions are also controlled by your subconscious mind. That's why at times you might feel afraid, anxious or down without wanting to experience such a feeling.

The subconscious mind vividly stores your past life experiences, beliefs, memories, skills, situations you've been through and all images you've ever seen. It stores everything that is not in your conscious mind.

A good way to understand the subconscious mind is to look at the example of a person learning to drive a car. At the beginning she wouldn't be able to easily converse with anyone while driving. Out of necessity she would be focusing her attention on learning and mastering the different moves and maneuvers involved in operating a vehicle. Conversation at this point would be a dangerous distraction for her. That's because at the start she still uses her conscious mind to drive. But over time as driving becomes more natural to her without having to think about it. This is because the skill of driving gets transferred to her subconscious mind thus freeing up memory in her conscious mind.

How to use the conscious and the subconscious minds together

There is a simple exercise that you can do in order to perfectly understand the difference between the conscious and the unconscious mind. Begin by controlling your breathing rate as if you are going to try to relax, holding your breath and then exhaling in a controlled manner. While you were controlling your breath your conscious mind was in charge.

Now stop controlling your breath and let it flow naturally. When you forget about this exercise you will notice how your subconscious mind returns your breathing rate back to its normal rate.

It's good to understand how both the conscious and the unconscious mind work together and then take advantage of their combined power.

When we blend the effectiveness of our sub conscious mind and the seamless power of visualization, it naturally becomes easier to train or control your mind. In the following section I talk about how to prepare your mind for the practice of Visualization.

Chapter 15: How Our Minds Work

We are all constantly thinking and the type of thoughts and ideas that fill a person's mind, will directly affect their actions and thus their circumstance in life.

Usually when people are asked to picture their mind, they think of the picture below ... a brain.

But the brain is just an organ in the body, which performs certain relaying functions to keep the body running properly. It is certainly a part of our mind, body, spirit, consciousness, but it is not our mind. The brain of Albert Einstein was examined and appeared to be like every other brain.

The workings of the mind are a complete mystery to over 90% of the population. It usually puts people in a state of confusion.

Because!

"Mind" Is an Activity Not A Thing.

On the next few pages I will show you what I have learned about how your mind works and explain how you can use your new knowledge, to change the results you are getting in your life.

Meet the "Stick Man"...

Most people find that "Stick man" gives them a picture to use, as they begin to understand the workings of their mind.

"Stick Man" was a concept originated by Dr. Thurman Fleet, of Santonio Texas in 1934. Dr. Fleet was the founder of a personal development technique called "Concept Therapy". The Stick Man has also been used by Bob Proctor and several others.

As you can see, the mind has two parts to it.

The Conscious Mind (CM) and
The Sub-Conscious Mind (SM)

Your Conscious Mind

This is the part of you that thinks and reasons. It is the one thing that separates "human" consciousness from the rest of the animal kingdom.

In your ability to "choose" your thoughts, reside free will and your power to create.

Your results in life are determined by the thoughts that you choose, but thinking, is influenced entirely by the content of your subconscious mind.

Who you are as a person, is in fact a reflection of the content of your sub-conscious mind.

Children's minds operate slightly different, as they don't form a conscious mind (beta brainwaves) until approximately 7 years old. This is a key point in how we become the person we are.

I'll explain in a minute.

Your Sub-Conscious Mind

The sub-conscious mind refers to all the mental activities or processes going on that we are not consciously aware are happening. This is where habits reside. This is where we keep all the automatic actions and reactions, like reaching for a cigarette or driving without thinking.

Your sub-conscious mind is like a huge recording device that records everything that you see, smell, hear, taste and feel. We also have a sixth sense which you might have experienced.

In fact, the subconscious mind can recognize, file, store and retain 100 million pieces of information per second!

Think of it like this:

If you were to take a walk through the busiest part of the center of a city, such as, Paris or Chicago, at lunch time, on a weekday, it would record all the shops, what was in the shops, all the cars, their color and type and every person, what they were wearing, even the expressions on their faces.

It records absolutely everything including your feelings, thoughts and emotions!

As grown-ups, we have developed mental filters, we only consciously notice the things we decide to focus on, but your subconscious mind gets everything!!

It is a fact that each and every one of us has the most powerful computer that ever existed right between our ears, and it is believed by some scholars that even the most intelligent people don't even use 5% of its power.

And here is what happens to your computer...

It gets mis-programmed!

And this is how it happens....

To fully understand how this happens, we need to have a look at the evolution of the mind from childhood to adulthood.

When a child is conceived, a consciousness forms and that consciousness has a subconscious mind. At this point the subconscious mind is empty.

Most people believe that a child begins to learn when it is born, although some believe the child begins to learn in the womb.

Any way you look at it, the acceleration of learning definitely begins once it has been born and has come fully into the physical world.

The child, like an adult, begins to receive information from all of its senses. i.e. Sight, hearing, smell, taste, touch and I believe also a sixth sense. This is when you begin to develop your self-concept.

The two drawings will give you a visual concept of what is happening.

We all know that a child's mind is impressionable, but exactly how impressionable?

When a child is born, it has a Pure and Clean Mind....It's like a blank sheet of paper.
When you are young, the people around you, such as parents, uncles and aunts,

brothers and sisters, give you direct commands. The commands are something like this:

"Don't do this" or "don't do that" or "No! You can't do this" or "No!, You can't do that".

The word that parents use the most is "No".

"Researchers estimate that an average child receives at least 20 negative messages from their parents for every positive, reassuring one."

Secondly, they talk about you, in front of you as if you weren't there, and say things like:

"He's a bad child"

"He doesn't get along well with other children"

"He's such a pain, he's always crying"

"She's such a noisy child, she just won't shut up".

And when you get older they say things like:

"She is just not very coordinated, she'll never be a dancer" or

"He's hopeless at math, he'll probably fail his exams again" or

"You're not smart enough to run a business, get a good job and let the company look after you."

All of this type of negative programming went straight into your subconscious mind...

I repeat - They went STRAIGHT into the extremely impressionable subconscious mind.

For the most part we have no idea what programming went in. We just know the child will unknowingly accept it as truth.

Of Course, they also said good things... but they're not enough.

Everything that you felt, heard and saw is also stored in your subconscious mind and I mean everything.

It records all of the television, the radio, the books, the comics and any other information that you came in contact with.

It records what your brothers, sisters, aunties, uncles, teachers and friends said.

But most importantly...

Please pay special attention to what I am going to say next...

The subconscious mind records and highlights any information "The Child" is exposed to, which has an emotional nature to it, such as,

"You have to work hard, to make it"

"Hard work is rewarded"

"Money doesn't grow on trees"

"You have to work hard for money"

"We're poor but happy"

"I hate my job, but I've got no choice"

"We have to stay together for the children"

"Everyone who has money, must have deceived somebody"

"Only evil people have money"

"Rich people are people who have ripped everyone off"

"You have to go in early and come home late, before you can come in late and go home early"

The word "e-motion" is short for energy in motion and although the child may not yet understand words or meanings of words – it can easily register energy and the emotion of what is being said.

All this takes place from the moment you were born to age 7 and is known as the "Imprint Years" and at around seven, the "conscious" mind is formed. At this point, the scientists would say the mind starts making beta waves and they start to make decisions or judgments about whether something is true or not.

All the information, ideas and feelings that we are exposed to in the "imprint years" become state bound and out of our awareness. State bound means that for the memory to come back into our awareness, we would have to get back into the same mental state we were in when it occurred. For that reason, it remains in our master file of feelings, ideas, sights and sounds, but we are not aware it is there. This master file is used by our computer mind to make interpretations of events and decisions concerning their meaning. Our reaction to the events of our lives then determines how we live our lives. All this is said to be unconscious or subconscious.

New programming, whether good or bad, continues for the rest of your life, but the foundations are pretty much set in the first 21 years and the old programming will continue to run you until you make a decision to change it, find out how to change it, and most importantly – Do the work to change your mind or old programming!!!!

During your first 21 years, you become a set of conditioned responses, emotions, attitudes behaviors and values. This is where you basically become you, your beliefs, your values, your personality, or who you are.

The elephant is a good example of negative imprint training. Let's look at how it is done. Have you ever been to the circus and saw a huge elephant being controlled by a small chain attached to a small stake stuck in the ground? It is so obvious that the elephant could easily pull the stake and be free!

Yet, the elephant doesn't do it, because when he was a baby, the trainer put a big chain on his leg, with a big stake stuck in the ground. Regardless how much the little elephant pulled, he could not get free. This taught the elephant it was useless to try to get free. This becomes so strong in the elephant's mind ... that they have been known to burn to death in a tent fire because they thought it was useless to pull on that stake.

"We all live in a box of our own making

The problem is the directions for getting out of the box

Are printed on the outside of the box."

(Unknown)

Like the elephant, it is not the events in our lives that shape us, but our beliefs as to what those events mean. This makes the whole process more complicated and for that reason it is not easily understood. Each individual builds their own box.

In his book, "Awaken the Giant Within" Tony Robins relates this story "He was bitter and cruel, an alcoholic and drug addict who almost killed himself several times. Today he serves a life sentence in prison for the murder of a liquor store cashier who "got in the way". He has two sons, born a mere eleven months apart, one of whom grew up to be "just like Dad" a drug addict who lived by stealing and threatening others until he, too, was put in jail for attempted murder.

His brother however, is a different story' a man who's raising three kids, enjoys his marriage, and appears to be truly happy. As a regional manager for a major national concern, he finds his work both challenging and rewarding. He's physically fit, and has no alcohol or drug addictions!

How could these two young men have turned out so differently, having grown up in the same environment, virtually? Both were asked privately, unbeknownst to the other. "Why has your life turned out this way?" Surprisingly, they both provided the exact same answer: "What else could I have become, having grown up with a father like that?"

So, often we're seduced into believing that events control our lives and that our environment has shaped who we are today. Some people believe it is their parent's fault that they are not living a life of abundance. No greater lie was ever told! It's not the events of our lives that shape us, but our beliefs as to what those events mean.

I had an interesting experience a few years ago. It happened that several of my siblings and I met a few days before the family reunion. We rented a van and made a pilgrimage to our home town and the home where we grew up. The most amazing thing was each person had a different view of events that happened, as we were growing up. Sometimes, I thought we must not be talking about the same experience.

What imprinted on our minds was the feelings we had about the event and often, our feelings differed greatly about the same event. The siblings, who were younger, might have experienced fear, while the older ones felt completely different about the same experience.

It was not the events of our lives that were imprinted, but our beliefs as to what those events meant. It was amazing!

"Change starts with a decision to make the change." Anthony Robbins

Chapter 16: Visualization Secret Technique

Set your mind on the things above, not on the things that are on earth. (Colossians 3:2)

Up until now we've talked about our purpose and desires, but now we need to find out how we can strengthen them in order to fit the prospect of a better self that is in accord with God's principles and happiness. There are certain proven techniques which we will be learning in this part in order to get the best out of our selves and be constantly on the path of happiness and faith.

Remember yourself as a sphere, as we talked in the previous chapter? That was a visualization technique. Its role is to strengthen your motivation towards healthy desires in order for them to become externalized healthy habits, to rewire your brain and to endow you with a certain sense of confidence, which all of us, more or less, need as much as we can. You'll see that you'll be more focused, more agile in your work and daily activities, and that it will be easier to project and manifest your desires and wishes, conditioned by the fact that they are true in their nature and evoke faith in their outcome.

This technique that we spoke of helps in bringing your mind in a state of calm and relaxation, eliminating stressful elements from your psyche and concentrating only on the ones which aretrue to your life's goal and principles. Everywhere around us, on the road, when we go to the supermarket to buy groceries, on the billboards, in the supermarket, on the television, on the internet, we find so much information that our brain is confused and it sometimes struggles to separate what is best for us and what is not. With their greedy modern marketing techniques, companies lie to us through the use of advertisements, and bombard our brains with useless information which are later manifested in false desires, auctioned unconsciously.

Visualize your goal, and try to constantly keep it in your mind, every day. Remember, always ask yourself, why do you desire this and that, and what is your true desire. Regain authorship. If your desire is high in its vibration, God will let His Will shine upon yours, strengthening it and blessing it. By praying and through constant thoughtfulness of our true desires, being present in the moment and focusing on its goal, we release ourselves from the daily stress and in the same time work towards a better life and a better future, with a healthy set of principles etched in our goals.

We must never forget that all external manifestations of our will always have an internal basis, rooted in our souls, and processed by our mind. Tune in to your higher vibrations and tune in to God's frequency. As we've discussed in Chapter 2, clear and true desires have stronger and truer outcomes. By realizing how much power God can bestow upon you to make the world better, to be His tool, is realizing to be happy.

By constantly providing yourself with daily positive affirmations, you can literally hack your brain, to put it in modern words. This technique can be easily empowered and achieved with the aid of prayers. Implement the power of daily asserting your true desires at the end of your prayer, and tell yourself in the presence of Providence how much your desire can benefit your fellow sisters and brethren, if fulfilled. As you constantly tell yourself everyday day and visualize your intended goal in the confines of your mind and in the presence of God, your message will be selfconsciously accepted. Visualize it as you communicate it to the Higher Powers, feel it materializing and being blessed. Your desire, I repeat, if true and with good faith, will unfold for your benefit and for the ones dearest to you.

Divinity is present everywhere. Another example I give, for a better understanding of the earlier paragraphs, is this:

Imagine that the Voice of God is a tune, and we need to sing along this tune. Of course, if we want to sing along and be in tune, we need to be good singers, naturally. Good musicians and singers practice a lot, and this is what my point is. In our case, the World is God's own band, and each and every one of us is one of His singers. If we are noble in our actions, and practice good faith daily, we can be in harmony with the World and in the same time let others hear what 'good singers we are', and thus becoming an inspiration for them to become 'good singers', just like ourselves, and tuning in God's harmony.

Another technique is being grateful, stating each day, if possible in a written journal, why you are grateful for what you have at the current moment. Count your blessings, for short. Always keep God in your mind, concentrate on the happiness of your current moment. Smile that you are alive. Be grateful that the Light of Life shines through your body and warms your blood. Reflect on your life, reflect on the past times of sorrow and blow them away cheerfully and with a smile drawn upon your face, shining in the full rays of love and peace. Visualize your sphere of light as a part of a grater whole, infinite and unimaginable, but felt, just as the stars make you feel when you gaze upon them on the night's sky.

Visualization provides one of the most important requirements for the fulfillment of your desires and the achievement of your goals. Remember, each and every element of the World God created has a mental correspondence, an unseen seed which, if tended with enough care and attention, sprouts forward your truest goal and wish.

Chapter 17: Key Points In

Visualization

Visualization helps you create your own reality and achieve your desired success in life. Here are key points in visualization that will help you manifest your dreams into a physical reality.

• The pictures that you create in your mind have an impact your life and the actions that you take.

• When you visualize, you activate the parts of your brain that is responsible for carrying out your actions.

• The subconscious mind is excellent when it comes to reverse engineering due to its deductive nature. It can work wonderfully backwards going to the means.

• If you focus intently on a single goal in your mind, your subconscious will automatically help you find the means and information that are needed to achieve your goal.

• You don't necessarily need to know how to get to your goal. Your subconscious mind will help you with that.

• It is important and necessary that you are able to feel and see your goal as if it already happened when you visualize it.

Many successful people have used this technique either consciously or unconsciously. When using visualization to achieve your goal, remember to be clear with your intention, avoid any distractions and experience your intention or ultimate goal as if it already happened or it is already a done deal.

Chapter 18: Energy Clearing Techniques

As you learn about creative visualization, you may occasionally encounter blocks that prevent you from achieving your best, and it's important to recognize these blocks and eliminate them systematically in order to visualize properly and have the best results from your visualizations.

Blocks work by obstructing the energy flow, which subsequently impedes your progress. These blocks are usually caused by suppressed emotions such as self-criticism, resentment, guilt, fear and sadness. These emotions take a toll on your mental system, which causes it to tighten up, leading to the shutdown of your spiritual, emotional, mental, and even physical energies. Like with any other barrier, the only solution is to remove the obstacle and resume with the free flow of energy. Here are the key requirements to achieving this:

*You must first accept your current feelings, both emotionally and mentally. Acceptance will help you relax physically.

*You must then identify the problem clearly, as well as the core issue.

*When you start dealing with a part of your consciousness in which you have a block, you must experience and immerse yourself in the emotions that are suppressed and locked up in that area, in a way that's amicable, loving and capable of acceptance.

Doing this will not only unblock the trapped energy, but it will also give you the unique opportunity to watch and experience your underlying negative attitudes, thought processes and beliefs that caused the block in the first place.

When you isolate these processes, you can observe them clearly and then eliminate them.

The difficulty disappears as soon as you acknowledge and accept yourself as you are. You have to accept and love yourself compassionately for preserving these attitudes and beliefs, but you also have to gather the mental courage to release them because they are very untrue, destructive, self-defeating, and virtually debilitating.

Here are some of the attitudes and beliefs associated with most people, and that are very troublesome.

*I am not fine... I believe that there is something terribly wrong with me... I'm very unworthy and undeserving.

*I've done terrible things in my life, and I believe that I must be punished for the same.

*Everyone in the world, myself included, are greedy, foolish, stupid, sinful, untrustworthy, selfish and cruel.

*The world is a very dangerous place. There is scarcity of love, good things and money, and therefore, I must fight and toil for my due share or there's no hope that I'll ever get enough for my needs in this life or if I have an excess of something, it means that there's someone else who has to go without it.

*Life is painful, suffering, hard work... there's no space for fun or pleasure.

*Love is injurious and hazardous, and I might even get hurt

*Power is unstable, and I might end up hurting someone

*Money is the root of all evils, as well as the cause of corruption.

*We live a dysfunctional world, and it will remain so.

*I do not have much control over what is happening in my life. I also feel vulnerable and powerless to do anything about the issues in my life and the state of affairs in the world.

Scan through the ideas above and see whether any of them is applicable to you, and if they are a reflection of your very own belief system.

The fact is that most people have had at least one of the mentioned thoughts. As such, you have all integrated negative thought processes in your perception of the reality, though the degree of this negativism varies from person to person.

These thought patterns have become a crucial part of your perception of reality over time, and these negative thought patterns are extremely active, seeking to influence your world presently. You should understand that these things are only your beliefs, and subsequently have no objective reality or truth. As such, the most effective tool you have to lead the change is to change and alter your own beliefs about nature of life, people, and reality, and then start acting according to the modified thought processes.

We will now look at some of the best clearing exercises.

If you are having difficulties and obstacles in achieving your goals, or you experience internal barriers that prevent you from accomplishing your best, then here is an exercise you can try:

1. Find a sheet of paper and write, "The main reason why I don't have what I want

and desire is...,"Proceed by jotting down all the thoughts that spring to mind in order to complete the sentence. Avoid spending too much time on the thinking as you may end up manipulating your real inner thoughts to something that's more appealing and easy to accept. Do not put much thought into what you've written. Ideally, you should end up with a list of 20 to 30 things. Here is a sample:

The main reason why I don't have what I want and desire is:

*I cannot afford it

*I'm too slothful

*It doesn't exist in the first place

*My parents said that I didn't have the abllity to do it

*I've failed in my previous efforts

*It's very difficult

*I'm not interested in doing it

*It's a bit too much for me

*My friend _____ wouldn't like that

*I'm scared of doing it

2. Repeat the same exercise, but with a twist this time. Here, you will specify the limitations of what you want or desire. For instance, "The main reason why I am unemployed is...," and then continue with the steps as before. List down everything you think is responsible for you being unemployed. Go through the list; look at it with a cool and calm mind, without any bias. See if there's any specific point that you think is particularly true for you.

Trying gauging the effect of these limitations on yourself and your world in general.

List down all the negative attitudes or thought process that you have about both yourself and others; other people, your relationships, life and the world at large. Next, analyze the contents carefully, and try to overcome the thoughts and ideas that consciously or unconsciously tend to hold control over you.

In case your emotions overwhelm you during this exercise, do not resist them. In fact, you should accept them as a vital part of your thought process and try to experience them as much as you can. This phase might also be associated with flashbacks about your past. This is because your parents and teachers told you something when you were young that shaped your perspective of the world in a certain way.

3. When you feel that you've completed the whole process and have gotten in touch with your negative beliefs and thought processes, you need to tear and discard the piece of paper. This is to symbolize that you are ready to let go and move on from those rigid beliefs and thoughts. Now, relax and repeat some affirmations in order to enforce the more open, constructive and positive thoughts to replace the negative ones.

Here are some positive affirmations that might come in handy:

*I am utterly free of my past

*I have gotten rid of all the negative and limiting beliefs, and they no longer have control over me

*I now want to forgive and release everyone in my life. Everyone is now free and happy.

*I do not have to please others intentionally because I'm very likeable in everything I do

*As of now, I have released all the disappointments, grudges, fear, resentment, and guilt that I had gathered in my life.

*I've dissolved all the negative self images and attitudes, and I now love and appreciate myself. Every obstacle that prevented my delight and full expression of life is no longer there.

Energy Clearing Exercises

#Release

The main idea behind this exercise is forgiveness and letting go of things.

1. Take a piece of paper and write down a list of all the people you think have caused you harm, have not treated you well, have been unjust to you, or whom you simply resent.

2. Beside the name, specify what the person did to bring you harm or the reason for your dislike towards them.

3. Next, close your eyes gently and relax. Imagine each of the persons mentioned in the list, and have a small conversation with them individually, explaining that although they had previously hurt your feelings, and made you angry, you are now ready to let go and forgive them, and bring down all the differences you had between yourselves. Finish by blessing the person. "I release and pardon you. You can go on with your own life and be happy." This will help you unblock the energy that had been trapped, and use it for more productive purposes.

4. Finish by saying, "I forgive and release you all" and then discard that piece of paper.

This process helps lighten the load of emotions you have been carrying for many years, and start with the process of forgiveness. The most interesting part is that your effect is passed on to others. This means that when you forgive the people included in that list, even if you are not in direct contact with each other, they will pick up the signal subconsciously, and enable them to clean up their lives.

The first time you do this might not make you feel satisfied or relieved by the process. This is particularly true for certain people, such as your parent, spouse, or any other significant person in your life. This is because these people tend to induce very strong emotional responses, and you in turn, tend to suppress the feelings associated with them. The best advice here is to conduct the process in a secluded area in order to effectively and sincerely express your feelings as they are.

The most important takeaway from this process is to understand that you should never force forgiveness on yourself if you are not ready to accept your feelings or let go. Only when you accept and express your feelings can you really start the process of reconciliation. Repeating this process frequently will resolve the issue with time. Always keep in mind that you are doing this process for your own health and happiness. When you clean up your mind and your internal thought patterns, you are also able to boost your mental and physical energy.

#List of forgiveness

Here, you do the exact opposite; i.e. list down the names of all the people you believe you have hurt, committed an injustice against, or were generally not nice to them.

1. Start by closing your eyes and relax completely. Start picturing everyone on that list, and inform them of the wrong you did to them. Ask for their forgiveness, and their blessings.

2. Have another picture of the person doing so. When you are through with this process, write this at the end of the page: "I have forgiven myself and absorbed myself of all type of guilt!"

3. Complete the process by tearing up the piece of paper and then get rid of it.

Chapter 19: Power Of Imagination

Imagination is very powerful if you only know how to use it well. Many people use the Law of Attraction but they often wonder why they get what they don't want rather than what they want. Let us look at this way; they often imagine their past experiences which is their reality. The bad experiences that happened keep on repeating in their minds, that the LOA will allow these to happen again. It is better to imagine what still hasn't happened and visualize what you want to be in any situation. The most dominant thought in your mind will eventually show itself.

The bad things happen because we focus on them without even knowing it. The more that we regret and keep on remembering them, the more they will keep coming back.

We should change our perspectives; imagine our aspirations even if these haven't happened yet. Just keep on repeating in your head the things that you want in life and these will turn to reality. You may not notice it yet, but gradually the effects of your imagination will show. As you keep on doing this, your life will grow with it!

How often do you live and feel your dreams? It is harder and would require more energy to imagine the life that hasn't happened yet. But if you keep on imagining and visualizing your aspirations, you will eventually attract opportunities. It also applies to when you always complain why you don't have this and that; the LOA will block the opportunities. It is because you concentrate on what you don't have with those complaints.

We see what people do but not what they imagine. When they experience positive circumstances we often say they are lucky, but we really don't know what they think and imagine at times.

Each time we say that many things happen by chance but what we actually mean is that we can't understand and explain how these things happen.

Chapter 20: How To Use The Sub-Conscious To Succeed

Now that you know what the sub-conscious is, how it works and how to tap into it, it is time to put all the things you learned to good use. Think about a particular goal that you want to achieve. For illustration purposes, let's say you want to learn how to skydive.

When setting a goal, it is important to keep it rational. A goal to learn how to actually fly like a bird is irrational, but skydiving is the closest you can get to flying and something that you will be able to achieve. Unfortunately, you are afraid of heights and you have seen too many people die during a dive. How do you deal with this fear by harnessing the power of your sub-consciousness?

1.   Know what you want and focus on it

So you want to be able to skydive. Focus on it and don't expand your thoughts to parasailing or overcoming claustrophobia.

How you deal with your sub-conscious with regards to skydiving will be different from working out your fear of enclosed spaces. The approach may be similar, but the thought process will be different. The idea is to focus on one goal at a time.

2.   Identify the sub-conscious patterns that keep you from reaching your goal

What is preventing you from going out of your comfort zone? Is it the fear of falling, the thought of the parachute failing to open, or the idea that you might get tangled with your harness when you are about to jump? It is vital that you talk to yourself with all honesty, without excuses or masks, the very reasons that you harbor doubts and fears. In the event that you can't seem to find the answer, you can always talk to a friend or get professional advice from a therapist.

The reason that you need to identify the obstacles or blocks of your sub-consciousness is for you to be able to openly communicate with it. If you are able to build a communication system between yourself and your sub-conscious mind, the easier it will be to deal with your fears, anxiety or other reasons that make you chicken out of a skydive.

3. Practice sub-conscious shifting methods at bedtime

15 minutes before going to sleep, your body and mind will reach that state of relaxation, where you feel your muscles loosen up, your breathing relaxes, your heartbeat slows down, and you feel calm all over. Think of this 15-minute window as similar to meditation, where your sub-conscious is open to receive messages. Conveying a message, however, can be a bit tricky and may require practice of any of the four communication methods.

• Use of metaphors

Because of the huge impact that metaphors have on the sub-conscious, they are said to be an effective communication tool. In your case, imagine yourself as a plane flying high in the sky, past and over huge clumps of clouds. Flying without fear or thought of any negativity. To make it easier to re-program your sub-conscious, put on relaxing music and then start thinking of metaphors once your mind is calm and relaxed.

Using metaphors, however, is applicable to people who love to daydream, have an artistic personality and have the tendency to use metaphors when talking or dealing with other people. Are you one of them?

• Visualize the end result

While in a calm and totally relaxed state of mind and body, think about that goal that you so deeply desire to achieve, which is skydiving. Then, create an image of how your life is going to be when you finally succeed, think about the end result. Pay attention to every element that makes the image real rather than imagined, such as the sound, colors, scent of the open air, or the people around you, congratulating your success and giving you a pat on your back. Or it could be just the pilot of the plane giving you the thumbs up. This refer to a video visualization of the final result.

Afterwards, focus on one memorable image that you want to frame and remember for as long as possible. What you are doing is static visualization. You can then mix both video and static visions, switching your view with one from the other. Repeat this pattern every time you go to sleep for the next 21 days and the entire process will become easier to do.

• Use good memories of the past

Think of a past memory that made you feel good and relive the actual experience in your mind. When you succeed, you will be able to establish a connection with your sub-conscious. If any of the negative memories creep in, chuck them out right away. Because allowing them into your sub-conscious will have a damaging effect and you are unlikely to achieve your goal of skydiving without the fears or worries. Focus all your energy on the good memories, and think of one that you can relive over and over again.

• Anchor on affirmations

Do you still have that good memory that makes you feel good? Think about it again and think back to the very moment where you are about to reach massive excitement, fulfillment or happiness. Just when you are about to reach the climax, so to speak, implant that image and intense feeling into your sub-conscious. Feel your entire body responding to the image, the way it makes your spine tingles or the way you smile in great joy.

This method is the most important since you get to create a physical link to existing neurotransmission. As you reach that sense of intense excitement and the impulse goes past the synaptic cleft, a protein is released along with neurotransmitters, creating a memory that is more intense and has emotions.

Sleep should be a good time to visualize better things, situations and the like. So make a habit of reminiscing good memories. While you're at it, count back slowly from 100 to 1 and, at every few numbers, tell yourself"I am brave","Courage is all around me","I will brave it out and jump out of a plane". Every time you tell yourself something positive, you are planting the seed of new sub-conscious patterns, and every time you repeat the process, you nurture the seed to grow and become a sprout that will take roots.

4.   Be grateful always

People who accept their fate and feel grateful for what they have or where they are now have better outcomes than those who don't. Think about it; if you wake up every day angry with your lot in life, you will never find ways to make your life better. You will end up blaming other people, and completely overlooking the fact that you are alive, you have a family who support you, and friends who will be there if you need them. If you shut them out, the more miserable you will become. So, rather than allow your sub-conscious to focus on the thought of"I am poor", or"I will be miserable all my life", tap and program it with positive thoughts.

Now that you know what you want and focus on it, remove sub-conscious mind blockages, and mastered sub-conscious shifting methods, how will it help you turn your dream of skydiving into reality? It changes your perception about the activity and eliminate the negatives that you often surround with it. When you do, you also free yourself from the struggles you experience every time you try to get on a plane and decide to take a leap. With your sub-conscious programmed and re-wired, you will have the courage and the drive to skydive.

The idea behind harnessing the power of your sub-conscious mind to reach your goals and dreams is to create new programs in this part of your brain in order to change your personality or fix whatever problems it has. Think of your sub-conscious as the program that makes computer applications run. Every time an action is required, the program is retrieved and made to run. If it is corrupted in any way, the action will not happen. In the same sense, if the programming in your sub-conscious has many negatives instead of positives, your life could be unhappy and full of struggles. Why would you want that?

Chapter 21: Setting Goals-The Epitome Of Self-Growth:

How to Create Smart Achievable Goals

Earlier, we saw a few of the reasons why our lives stagnate. We also looked at a few reasons why we should avoid stagnation and procrastination despite its bed being ghostly beautiful and alluring.

We also looked at personal development. We defined what it is and looked at how it can help you take back control of your life. While doing this, we stated that personal development is your desire, will and active participation towards being the best YOU possible.

One of things we touched on is your courage to get started and your motivation to keep going even when the bed of stagnation and procrastination alluringly and teasingly invite you in.

Let's be honest for a minute, if you're reading this, it's either because your life is a bit stagnant or your life seems a bit repetitive and you would like to do something about it. Here is what no one out there is going to tell you while you can read all the personal motivational books you can find online and offline; personal motivation is not something you can find in a book. Sure, books will motivate and give you ideas on how to approach and pursue personal excellence; they cannot make the decision for you. Which decision is that?

"The decision to be better or the decision to relentlessly pursue personal excellence"

Therefore, the first key step to getting out of your comfort zone aka stagnation or eliminating procrastination is making the decision to get started on being the best YOU possible. The best way to do this is by setting goals.

We shall not define what goals are. However, what we shall mention the importance of setting them and consistently pursuing their achievement consciously and subconsciously.

Goal setting is an essential pillar to personal development. Again, as we have seen, personal development is pursuit of personal excellence. If you're not setting goals and actively pursuing them (remember pursuit can be conscious, i.e. any activity geared towards the attainment of goals, or subconscious i.e. using your subconscious mind to manifest desired goals), your life is stagnant and is thus likely to suffer from procrastination.

How does procrastination manifest? Well, it does so as thousands of unfinished projects and a haphazard approach to the pursuit and attainment of life goals all meant to give you the 'life you desire' as illuminated in the creative visualization exercise we practiced earlier. To achieve the life you desire, you have to set goals that drive you towards the attainment of the life you desire and actively pursuing these goals.

For example, to use personal development to stop procrastination or rid your life of stagnation, you need to set goals that drive you towards the opposite of your current situation. A good example of this is: let's say your life feels a bit stagnant and bland.

Fortunately, most of us know the importance of setting goals. Unfortunately, most of us don't know how to set SMART GOALS, i.e. most of us don't know how to set goals and actively pursue them.

Unfortunately, the world is full of people who work hard but never seem to get anywhere despite having set goals. The reasons for this are up for debate. However, one reason stated repeatedly is a failure to think about what you want in life.

Goal setting in personal development is the process in which you visualize your ideal future, and find the motivation that drives you to the attainment of that future.

What Is Goal Setting- is it Important?

Goal setting is the process of choosing an ideal future and clearly outlining this future then allocating your energy resources (mental or physical effort) to all undertaking that may bring about the ideal future.

Setting goals is the nerve center of any achievement you see around you. It is so important that every successful athlete, business people, and just about any top achiever you know or want to emulate uses it.

The aspect of setting goals allows you a wider-berth view of your long-term vision and provides you with short-term motivation to pursue the attainment of personal excellence.

When you set clearly defined goals, it is easier to measure their completion and success. When you complete a small goal, regardless of how miniscule it is, it boosts your confidence and motivates you towards the pursuit of other goals that may bring about your ideal future.

As stated earlier, most of us know the importance setting smart goals (fortunately).

If your life is stagnant or if you're procrastinating, then set SMART goals aimed at achieving the very opposite of this i.e. an exciting life and productivity. How do you go about setting smart goals? Let's look at that.

Chapter 22: Watch A Video Clip

What I found very useful is to view a video clip prior to beginning visualization. There was once I was holidaying and I was in this mall where there was a fashion show in the mall. The models are gorgeous and they are modeling in wedding and night gowns. I took a couple of video clips in close view on the models that I was attracted to and clearly what I would have wanted as a girlfriend.

If your goal is to go on a holiday and stayed in a comfortable hotel, I have this tip for you. I was on a holiday trip in Shanghai and although the client has put me up in an average hotel but it was a suite! Now I have stayed in many hotels before, staying in a suite was my first.

I felt excited the moment I walk into the room... well a suite! It has a bedroom with TV, dressing table, closet, bathroom like the usual hotel room. But this is only a third of the total area of the suite. There is also a large living room with another TV and a big sofa set. The living room was so spacious that the TV and sofa set occupy only one half of the living room.

The other half of the living room has a round dining table with chairs. Additionally there is the kitchen with refrigerator and cooking appliances. So it is like a house. It is on the 43 floor and the view was fantastic. I took out up my phone and took video, talking as I walked around the suite. Guess what I uttered at the end of the video as the camera pointed to the view below.

Hence this video taken with my voice describing the scene as I walked around the suite ending with a Wow! This video greatly aided my visualization of being able to achieve this with my own paid holiday.

Chapter 23: Creative Visualization

The Key to Success is to Practice and then Practice Again and Again. Set aside a time each day to do your creative visualization exercise. It is best if you can do it once in the morning and once before bed. You will see your life transforming in a miraculous way once you have mastered the 5 step process.

Get On With Your Day. Once you have completed your exercise get on with the rest of your day. Count up from 1-5 to bring yourself to a level of conscious where you are fully awake. At the bed time exercise it is preferred that you wake yourself fully from the visualization exercise before going to sleep.

Let the Universe Handle the How. You must not focus your visualizations on the process but on the outcome. Accepting that you are one with the Universal mind you will be able to release any need to control the process.

You Can Take Inspired Action. You must be calm and deliberate in the actions you take knowing that they are taking you closer to the outcome that you desire. Remember to follow your natural instinct and listen to your intuition.

Feedback for the Mind. The more feedback you offer your mind the easier it will internalize and accept a new concept. Once you get to the point where you believe in the process in practice and not just the theory then you are pretty much ready to create anything you choose. As a beginner you should try and manifest a blue feather using the basic visualization steps to imagine a blue feather. Try and think about it as often as you can for 2 to 3 days. You will experience a blue feather in some way in your physical world within a short period of time. If you do not see the feather come back to it at another time just persevere do not get frustrated. Creative visualization is basically your ability to consciously create your ideal reality. Master the five steps in creative visualization relax, imagine, feel, believe, and detach.

Chapter 24: An Inner Inventory:

Where Are You Now?

Here's an opportunity to look a little deeper into yourself.

Think about how you feel about yourself and your life in the following areas, then write down your responses.

Describe Yourself and Your Life in These Areas:

- Education
- Work
- Friends
- Family
- Physical Self
- Emotional Self
- Strength/Talents
- Partner/Mate

- Personality
- Finances
- Confidence
- Possessions
- Happiness
- Success

Chapter 25: Using The Law Of Attraction To Attract Success

Success means something different to each of us. Someone may define it as having more money whereas for another person, success may mean being more spiritual or enlightened. Whichever way we choose to define it, being successful in one or more aspects of our life is something we all yearn for. Be it spirituality, happiness, relationships, professional life, business, health, fitness, or something else, we want to enjoy success in the aspects of life that hold importance for us.

While being successful may seem difficult, in reality it is not that difficult. You just need to have the right mindset to harness the power of LOA to attract success towards you and then consistently work hard for it.

Here are some LOA hacks that can help you manifest this goal easily.

Know What You Want

Just as is the case with love and money, be clear on the type of success you wish to have. Spend quality time with yourself and think about the sort of success you want right now or the goal you would like to achieve first. You can have multiple goals on your list; do not feel bad for wanting to achieve many goals. Write them down and then pick one you feel strongly about right now and want to achieve as soon as possible.

Ask yourself questions such as:

1)   "In which direction would I want to direct my life?"

2)   "Where am I headed and where do I actually want to go?"

3)   "What is the one thing that brings true happiness and meaning into my life?"

4)   "What is the purpose of my life?"

Reflect on these and similar questions and use them to figure out what you want. Additionally, when thinking about your goal, consider your likes, interests, dislikes, passions, and talents. Sometimes because we are so close to it we can't see it for ourselves. If that is the case, ask your family, friends and coworkers to let you know what they think you are naturally good at. Think about what you would want to be doing over anything else if money and time were not issues. What is your passion or calling? What gets you excited to get out of bed in the morning? When you are clearer on what you want, create a goal based on it followed by a plan of action so you know what you want and how to go about fulfilling that goal. Make sure to give your goal a deadline so you know when it is due and can starting working on it timely.

Think About Your Goal as Much as Possible

Create your 'goal board' and spend about 15-minutes of your day thinking about it. Visualize achieving that goal and practice positive affirmations based on it. Moreover, whenever you pursue a task or step that takes you closer to your goal, visualize yourself doing each step of the process and celebrate your accomplishments along the way. For example, if you intend to create a presentation for a meeting, think about how you will prepare it, the research you will conduct, how you will review it, and so on. This helps you gain clarity on how to perform the task, improve your focus on it, and trains your mind to be actively involved in it while you do the work.

Naturally, when you focus better on your task, you perform better at it, which improves your chances of success - helping you draw more success towards you.

Feed Your Mind Positive Mental Thoughts

As important as it is to spend time with like-minded and positive people as a way to stay focused on your goal, it is equally important to feed your mind positive mental thoughts so it stays optimistic and focuses on your goal. Read books, listen to podcasts, watch videos focused on achieving your goals, do whatever it takes so you stay positive and constantly think about your goal. Follow those you admire in person and on social media and distance yourself from and unlike anything that brings you down or takes you farther away from your goals. This way, you will strengthen your ability to think positively and draw upon good experiences that help you fulfill your goal and become successful.

Take Action towards Your Goal

Unless and until you take any positive action towards your goal, you will not actually fulfill it. To become a well-recognized singer or to develop your own clothing brand or to become the best software developer in the world, you need to do something to achieve that goal. For that, you need to first have your plan of action. Unless you are clear on what you are supposed to do and how you are supposed to execute that step, you won't move closer to your goal and if you won't even move an inch towards your goal, you won't be able to actualize it.

To ensure you do not lose sight of your goal and actually fulfill it, come up with a detailed plan of action that clearly describes the steps you need to take to meet your goal. Break your long-term goal into a mid-term and short-term goals. Next, take the short-term goal and chop it into smaller parts and pieces that give you a better idea of how to fulfill that goal. For instance, if your long-term goal is to become a popular singer, you need to first become a recognized singer in your community or city. Now think of how you can achieve this short-term goal. List down those many things you need to do to achieve your short-term goal and then combine those steps to create your action plan for now.

Go through each step and write down how to execute it. If you are supposed to gain recognition as a local singer, you can build your presence on social media, participate in local singing competitions, and meet more singers etc. to achieve your goal.

When you have an action plan, start following it without wasting any more time. If the first task is to upload a video singing a song, do it now. If you need to attend a social gathering where you can meet people who can help you in achieving your goal, do that. The more steps you take towards fulfilling your goal, the closer you will move towards achieving the success you actually want. Continuous action in a positive direction creates great momentum!

When working on your goal, make sure to record your performance in different tasks and activities to become better aware of your strengths, weaknesses and accomplishments. This way you know what areas to improve on and what areas to use/exploit to achieve your goal faster. Don't let your areas of improvement stop you, however. We all aren't naturally great at everything. Instead of taking the time to personally learn the task at hand, enlist friends, hire a coach, or outsource help to get you past that hurdle as soon as you can and closer to success.

On this journey, you will face some hardships and falter at times. During these times, it will be easier for you to stop believing in yourself and feel that you are not worthy of the success that you want. These are all the doubts in your head that will spark your inner critic to lash out. This is normal because that is how we feel and think in difficult times. Our brain is trying to protect us so anytime we try something for the first time it is going to seem difficult. However, you need not let these thoughts affect you and weigh you down in any way. In upsetting times, listen to the negative voices inside your head, acknowledge them and then let go of them by not holding on to them. Instead, listen to the voices, feel the fear and make a decision to do it anyway.

At the same time, practice your success based affirmations and visualize yourself achieving your goal. By doing this, you shift your focus from the upsetting situation to the present and your goal, and start focusing more on what you can do right now. This helps you get back up and make another effort to achieve what you want.

When working on the aforementioned strategies, track your performance by recording it in your journal. Go through these entries daily to review it and to check whether a certain strategy is working well for you. This helps you make necessary changes to your strategy and adjust accordingly.

Chapter 26: Other Things To Remember

Creative visualization is about changing your perception of the world around you and allowing positive energy to find you. It assists in programming your mind to be accepting of the success that you are looking for and to open your mind to new opportunities that can take you where you want to go.

Don't give up, even if it seems to be taking a long time for you to be getting where you want to be. Just keep practicing your skills and soon everything will open up for you.

When you combine the strength of your imagination, your new meditation skills and all of the positive energy held within you then you can easily manifest the things in your life that you deserve. Enjoy your new life!

Chapter 27: A Meditation Walk

Through

To most people in today's day and age, it can be hard to survive in the hectic lifestyle of business and social engagements and still have a chance to stop and smell the roses. But when we are making so many demands on our time and on ourselves, it can make it impossible for us to find the inner peace and balance that is essential to our well-being in order to find happiness.

The stress of everyday life can often feel insurmountable. When we have to surrender so much of our time and energy to tasks that may not necessarily serve us, it can make it difficult to make the time we need to allow ourselves to process what is going on in our lives and provide ourselves with comfort, peace, and a sense of loyalty to our own needs and desires.

When we are disconnected from our own needs and desires, that can pose a serious problem. If we aren't honoring ourselves in every way possible, that can make it difficult to move forward in the direction that we choose; making it difficult to serve our goals and work toward achieving our purpose.

Fortunately, there are many ways that we can allow ourselves to surpass the barriers that we construct during our daily lives so that we can begin to get in touch with who we truly are and the things that we really want and need in order to be the best versions of ourselves possible. Meditation has been utilized for thousands of years as a way to help us to get in touch with our inner selves and with the unshakeable truths that we

lock deep inside our unconscious minds.

Being able to tap into those things may seem divine to some, and practical to others. However, you choose to view meditation, there are many benefits to it that surpass any

162

bias you may have about it. Most people may be afraid to attempt meditation, thinking you have to contort yourself into an uncomfortable pretzel and try to listen to silence and stillness that seems impossible to maintain.

Most people have a very difficult time being able to sit still for long enough for meditation to make a difference. Our culture is generally discouraging of time to oneself, considering it selfish or unnecessary or antisocial. However, spending time on reflecting on one's life and circumstances may actually be one of the most necessary things one can do in order to master their destiny.

Meditation is actually easier than you might think. It can be easy to believe that there simply is no time to allow yourself to process, though this can sometimes result in insomnia as all the thoughts of the day that had been forced into repression begin to surface just as you are allowing your mind to relax and drift into a sleep. What most people don't realize is that during meditation, it is actually okay and natural to experience your thoughts and feelings. The trick is in simply allowing them to exist and to experience them fully so that they are able to move on.

We quiet our bodies and minds so that what we are dealing with can be experienced in a more genuine and pure form, so that these impressions and thoughts will not contribute to us staying stuck. When we are able to confront and face our thoughts and feelings, they no longer have as much power over us. And when we are able to truly begin to use meditation as a tool for self-exploration, it can provide us with insights that we may never have thought possible.

Meditation comes in many shapes and forms, and for people who have a hard time initiating meditation for themselves, it can be useful to seek out resources that can teach you more about how to use meditation. Many websites offer videos and tutorials that will help to guide you in empowering meditation strategies. There are also books and CDs out there that can be useful in undergoing meditation for beginners who may not feel confident undertaking it on their own.

The first thing you need to do for meditation to work for you is to put down all your pre-existing biases about it. Meditation isn't just something that weird hippies do in order to feel like everything is groovy. It is a useful tool that has helped to keep the mind and body aligned in the process of taking power over your actions and future. So, get that thought out of your head if it is there.

You should also know that meditation is not hard. In fact, it's the total opposite of difficult. All you really have to do is to make sure that you are comfortable and relaxed, preferably in a quiet space where you can focus on your breathing and allow your thoughts to come and pass as they naturally would. When you are in a relaxed state of mind, it is easier to see these thoughts and feelings in an objective way, and being objective to your own sensory input can provide you with deep insights about your body and your life.

For a beginner, meditation should be kept simple and comfortable. Get a cushion or a pillow that is very comfortable for you to sit on. You could even lie back if that suits you better. Once you are sufficiently comfortable, you should close your eyes and allow yourself to get relaxed. This is similar to getting ready for sleep as you allow your breathing to happen naturally and effortlessly. Don't get too caught up in not letting yourself have thoughts or emotions; the beginner's meditation should be kept simple.

Once you are comfortable with the practice of relaxing and clearing your mind, allowing your breathing to come as an organic process and not something that you are too fixated on, then you may begin to feel more comfortable delving into other types of meditation techniques. Meditation comes in many varieties, and if you are hoping to delve deeper into the meditation practice, then there are a few different directions that you could go in to do so.

Mindfulness meditation is one of the most popular forms of meditation, as mindfulness can be very helpful to anybody who is hoping to improve their life and feel more at peace. To undertake a mindfulness meditation, begin with the first steps outlined below. Get comfortable and relaxed. Next, allow yourself to become aware of your chest rising and falling as it breathes, and the feelings at the tip of your fingers and toes as you sit there. Contemplate the present moment and simply experience its wonder.

The way your fan may be humming, or the sound of the birds chirping outside, or the soft feeling of the surface you're sitting on. Allow yourself to take in all the little things about the moment that you are in right at that moment. This is how you succeed at mindfulness meditation.

This type of meditation can be utilized for people who have a difficult time staying grounded, and has actually been found to be helpful for people who have experienced certain types of trauma as well. It is a great way to help you to develop your mind and body connection if you find that it is something that you need to work on. You have to be fully aware of yourself before you can step into your dream vision. As mentioned before, nothing sabotages us quite as skillfully as we sabotage ourselves!

Another type of meditation is known commonly as concentration meditation. To perform concentration meditations, you focus your full attention on one single thing whether that thing is a specific area in the room, or something physical like the way that you are breathing. This type of meditation is very useful in problem solving or in helping you to get your mind off the things that are getting you down. When you focus on a specific thought or problem for too long, it can cause a lot of strain on the mind. By directing your thoughts and attention elsewhere, you are giving your mind a chance to interrupt negative thought patterns and anxiety to allow yourself a chance to recharge.

If you are a beginner, don't be too discouraged if it is hard for you to maintain your focus on the point that you have chosen for a long time. It takes a lot of practice to build up to maintaining your focus on a specific thing for a long period of time. Go ahead and go easy on yourself at first, starting in three-minute increments and gradually increasing that amount over time.

Concentration meditations help you to stay focused on one object or action so that it becomes easier for you to allow your thoughts to pass by you. It may help to imagine your thinking as a wave that should be allowed to wash over you and pass by without sweeping you away in it. They will come and go just like the tide, and when you are ready to return to them, you can. Until then, concentration meditations can provide you with a vantage point from which to view your thoughts objectively and gain insight into yourself and your life, providing you with a sense of empowerment that will truly grant you agency over your life and mastery over your dreams!

Goal: Take time out every day, starting with a simple three to five minutes, to meditate. Find a quiet, calm place in your home where you can allow yourself to close your eyes and get comfortable. Begin by simply closing your eyes and allowing yourself to feel confident in creating a safe and comforting space for yourself. Once you are pleased with this arrangement, you can begin trying more advanced types of meditation. Begin with a simple concentration meditation, where you close your eyes and focus on your breathing and your breathing alone. Thoughts may come to the surface, and that is okay. Simply acknowledge that they are there, and allow them to go on their way without trying to cling onto them. Do this with all your thoughts for about three minutes, until you can open your eyes, take a deep breath, and feel refreshed.

You can alternate between mindfulness meditations and concentration meditations as well, by closing your eyes, or even keeping them open, and focusing on the present moment and all the things you are feeling and experiencing at any given time.

Mindfulness meditations can be done anywhere at any time, so feel free to use them if you aren't feeling grounded!

Chapter 28: Common Pitfalls Of

Visualizations To Avoid

Enemies Of Visualization

The visualization is an essential element because it can bring a considerable difference in the success of a person. The best performance gets less affected by the distractions and extraneous incentives. You have to augment consciousness that there some elements that are enemies of visualization and can be a hurdle in your success path.

Concentrate On The Mechanics Of The Skills

Skill requires high competence, and then you should switch to the preconscious state of mind. Visualization on the execution of each movement may reduce the efficiency of the movement because it can reduce your visualization by diverting your attention to irrelevant tasks and targets.

Dwelling Of Internal Feelings And Ambiance Of Fatigue

It is important to keep an eye on the internal conditions by turning your visualization, but dwelling of these inner feelings is an enemy of external visualization. A man and woman require a common trait to avoid fatigue and pain during a workout for success. If you want to use your mind power, it is imperative to use visualization on the damage and get rid of fatigue. Distance from thoughts, such as injury, painful things and other thoughts will empower you to reduce the limitations and achieve big things.

Entertaining Nonproductive Self-Talk

Self-talk is an inherent feature of the conscious mind, but the nature and quality of the talk may differ. Negative self-talk can kill your performance and destroy your concentration. You should pay attention to the good thoughts because the fearful thoughts can reduce your confidence level. It is essential to use visualization on the positive and productive talks to maintain your visualization, execute yours the best moves and maintain motivation. It will be a powerful way to control your thoughts with the passage of time.

Visualization On The Past

If you want to maintain a healthy visualization, it is important to keep yourself fully engaged with the positive thoughts and actions. Your negative action and movements can be a killer for your visualization because your thoughts always remain engaged with the failures of past life and other irrelevant activities. It will reduce the motivation level and affect your performance. You have to use visualization on your present instead of engaging your thoughts in the experience. You should use visualization on the planning and risk management.

Visualization On The Future

Projecting your future and pondering on the outcomes of the task, as well as rewards, can obstruct your performance. If you want to enjoy a successful future, you should use visualization on your present and get rid of unnecessary thoughts about future outcomes. Control your concentration and do your best according to the demands by detaching you from the thoughts about outcomes.

Video And Audio Distractions

Social and electronic engagements can distract your attention because you may get distracted by different elements. It will be difficult to maintain visualization and attention because there are lots of elements to disturb your mind. You have to develop some concentrative skills by trying to eliminate distractions of your life. Get rid of distractions because these can kill your visualization. The electronic devices may tempt you to use them. If you want to use visualization, you have to turn off all electronic devices to reduce distractions with the beep of the message. Pay attention to your mental clarity because without it; you can't be able to maintain concentration and self-awareness.

Distractions

Distraction means the division of the attention of thoughts that can upset your concentration on regular activities. Your awareness can be troubled by an event, an object, group of people and visuals. If you lack the ability to pay attention, then it will be difficult for you to maintain visualization as well. There are lots of external and internal sources that can destroy your attention. Distraction is a mental state in which you find it difficult to maintain your visualization.

Chapter 29: My Income Is Continuously Increasing.

I am blessed to have an impressive income that is increasing each month. I am earning more money than I need.

As my income increases, I become even more confident in my ability to earn.

Making money comes easily to me. I continually find new income streams that add significant resources to my finances. There are thousands of ways to earn money, so I am confident I can make even more in the future.

My bank account is growing each day. It is exciting to watch my balance grow. I enjoy managing my finances.

I live a life of abundance. I am fortunate and grateful.

New opportunities to generate income are presented to me daily. My friends, associates, and even strangers, are a constant source of earning opportunities.

I am known as a person that can make things happen. As my reputation grows, I receive even more income-generating opportunities. My eyes are open to the possibilities that exist all around me.

The world is full of money. I am willing to do my part to earn my fair share. I am a money magnet.

Today, I know that small increases in income can grow into a large sum. I am looking forward to boosting my income today. My income is continuously increasing.

Ask Yourself...:

- What is my primary source of income? How can I add to that income stream?

- What financial opportunities do I have in my life right now?

- What would I do if I had a high income?

Visualize

waking to see additional funds in your bank account that were not there when you went to bed. Seeing yourself putting your skills into play to earn passive income. See yourself doing things you love that allow you to earn income that makes you feel as if you've retired.

Chapter 30: Manifesting Success

Being successful is one of the most sought after goals around. Who doesn't want to be great at what they do, and have others acknowledge that.

Again, the first hurdle that you have to jump is getting rid of the voice in your head that says you aren't quite good enough, and that you aren't going to be successful. That voice is wrong, and you know it is wrong; you just have to actively tell yourself that on a regular basis. Crush the voice that is spewing doubt and replace it with positive affirmations about yourself.

Let's say you want to be a successful business owner. You have ideas, but you don't know where to start. The first thing that you are going to do, after you squish those nagging doubts, is to accept yourself as a business owner. It doesn't matter what you are doing right now, in your life - if you're flipping burgers, you still have the ability, and the power, to become a successful business owner.

Visualizing yourself running a business you are passionate about. Let's use a flower shop for an example. If you wanted to run a successful flower shop - what would that entail?

This example lets you visualize very clear things. A successful flower shop will be filled with beautiful flowers of all varieties. You can close your eyes and picture dozens upon dozens of fresh roses; you can imagine how they would smell when they are brought out of the cooler, and placed on the working table. You can visualize the young lovers coming in to order those flowers for their sweethearts.

Take these steps over and over, spend a good amount of time, whenever you have it, visualizing yourself running this dream business. Picture yourself going to the bank to make deposits because your business is so very successful.

There are many different ways that you can visualize, but the more detail you can use, the more clear your vision will be and the more positive energy you will be sending out into the universe.

Don't forget to give thanks for the events that have gotten you to this point. Do you have an education, or do you have access to resources to give you the information you need to make your success happen? Those are great things to be happy and thankful for. They keep you focused on your goal while sending out the best vibrations related to your journey.

Really revel in the feelings that you have about doing what it is you dream about, and being successful in it. What kinds of emotions will this draw up for you? Accomplishment is a big one, starting to feel accomplished now will draw that accomplishment to you. Really feel like you have already achieved your goals for success.

When you start to slip, and have doubts, make sure that you replace those doubts with at least twice as many positive things about your goal, or yourself. This will help to keep you on track.

Don't walk blindly through your life. You need to pay attention to the things around you. If you aren't being actively involved, you won't notice when opportunities present themselves.

One final tip to help feel like you have already achieved your goals. Make yourself business cards with your new title, job, or business printed on them. It will give you something physical to hold on to and focus on and will make it easier to feel like you've already achieved your goal.

Chapter 31: Risk-Taking

Every great person in history has taken a risk. Rosa Parks took a risk by sitting in the "wrong" seat. Susan B. Anthony, Martin Luther King, Jr., Amelia Earhart and so many other important figures took risks. It is true that risks do not always have positive results, but that's why it is called a risk and not a guarantee!

Your first step to becoming a bonafide risk-taker is to understand that failure is inevitable. There will come a time when you feel insecure and you know that you have made a mistake. Keep rolling with the punches and you will soon find yourself working toward some semblance of success.

Next, determine if what you are doing is really a risk. What are you losing by pursuing a passion? Is it time? Money? Relationships? Assess the situation to determine exactly what is at stake. You might realize that the move isn't as risky as you thought it was, or perhaps you will realize that it simply isn't worth it.

Always bet smart. Just because you are taking risks does not mean that you have to be haphazard. You can judge whether or not the risk is worth it from afar. Above all, never make a decision when you are not at full capacity. Don't decide to do something simply because you are sad or upset. Think it through first so that you take only measured risks.

The reward of taking risks is to gain new opportunities. You will also soon find yourself becoming more confident with each successful risk that you take.

Chapter 32: What Is My Purpose?

It can be confusing to live in a world full of so many options, career paths and opportunities to know which one is best for us. There are going to be so many things that you like and dislike, and also things you have never experienced as of yet.

Instead of being caught up trying to seek a purpose, seek to let things be as they are and simply do the things that make sense to you at the present time. There is no measuring stick to say it's too late in life, and no rule book saying you should have found what you enjoy doing by now. It is also unwise to compare yourself to others. The other people in this world have different lives to you, and when you feel they have advantages, be aware they also have their disadvantages. Some people may appear to have their life sorted, well that should be great for them, but it doesn't help you by observing their life and thinking to yourself:

- "Why can't my life be that way?"
- "Why can't I figure out what I want to do, like them?"

Questions like these will bring you no closer to your answer. This takes your focus off what is important: living your life.

Time is moving fast and will not wait for you, every second lost cannot be regained, so stop wasting time asking pointless questions, and ask more positive ones, such as:

- "What are my talents?"
- "What would I really like to do in life?"
- "If I could have any type of lifestyle what would it be?"

- "What would be the perfect way for me to make a living?"

All of these questions are great to start with, but you can think of even more positive questions to help you discover what you truly want. You must answer honestly from deep within you, and not be influenced by other people. Also when answering these questions, do not think that anything is unrealistic; chose whatever it is that you want, even if it seems impossible at this moment.

Once you decide on a path you would like to take, you have to let go of the fear that stops you from doing it. Anything that is stopping you has to be abandoned; there is no time in life to worry. You just have to make bold actions. Worries are negative beliefs, which are not real. Anything you worry about is a pointless waste of energy.

You have to become fully focused on your new direction. As you do, you will gather more momentum and start to see results; this will reinforce your new beliefs and drive you towards your new destiny.

Chapter 33: Trump Outside Forces

Down

While it may be true that life isn't as easy as it seems and that it is never perfect, Stoics believe that it is what inside that counts. Seneca believed that people should not allow themselves to be penetrated by the world outside and that they should learn to see themselves as creatures who are strong and willing to move on with their lives.

This means that no matter what happens to you, and no matter what you might encounter in life, the way you deal with it is what matters. Yes, sometimes, life can be so tiring and you may feel that it is unfair, but if you choose to let negative thoughts rule your life then the more it means that nothing good will happen.

Why is that so?

Well, it may be a cliché, but when you see those failures and mishaps as challenges, you'd understand that you should still go on in life and you shouldn't let those things hinder you from becoming the person you want to be. Meanwhile, when you let negative thoughts rule your life, you're just allowing yourself to fall into a bigger hole of destruction even more.

Outside forces may knock you off, but it's up to you to stand up after each fall. You are always bigger than your circumstances.

Chapter 34: Write A Visualization

Script

Choose and focus on one or a few of your wishes and write a script, which will be the basis for what you visualize during the coming weeks. When this is your first project manifesting a wish with the Visualization System, choose a wish, which is easy to manifest.

It is best when you start and exercise with an easy wish, because you will program your system to get all you want. Your system should get used to it that your wishes are easy to be fulfilled. If you choose a wish, which is difficult to manifest, it will take much longer and it will be more difficult to manifest it, as if you start with an easy wish and built up on it. When you learn a music instrument, you don't start with a symphony, but with a short and easy to play melody.

1. Get to know the object or situation, which you want to manifest

Before you start writing the script, prepare yourself in getting to know better what you want. Find images of the object you want. Get all details about it. If possible, go to experience it with all your senses. See, touch, smell and hear it. For example, when it is a car, look at it from the outside and from the inside. How does it look and how does it smell inside? When you can test drive it, you will hear the sound of the engine. You will hear the sound of the radio, while you drive. Think about how you will feel when you own it.

2. Determine what role it will play in your life

Answer these questions in writing:

+ Which role does it play in your life, when this wish is fulfilled?

+ How important is it to you? Rate it with points between 1 and 10. Ten is very

   important and 1 is less important.

+ What will change in your life?

+ How will you feel right after your wish was fulfilled and how will you feel weeks

   and months later?

+ What will change in your life right after this wish was fulfilled and what impact

   will it have on your life months and years later? Will you still benefit from it in

   months and years or is it short lived?

Think of moments of your life, where this object or situation will make a difference. Describe these moments with a few sentences. Put emphasize on how you will feel.

3. Phrase affirmations regarding this goal or wish.

Think that an affirmation has to be positive. A "no" is not understood by your subconscious mind and it only knows the present tense.

Examples: "It is so great that I own this fabulous car." Or "I enjoy very much driving my new car."

"I am so proud that I have been promoted." Or "It feels great to have been promoted."

"It was a great decision to move to 'name of town or area'".

Make notes for your script:

Here an example

The goal: You want to earn $/€ 10.000 or more monthly.

When you earn $/€ 10.000 or more monthly, what will you do with the money, what will change in your life and how will you feel?

To earn more money you have to get active to give the money a chance to come into your life. Incorporate a money making activity into your script. Think, that you have to have joy doing it.

A: I moved to a larger apartment.

Living in a larger apartment means more space and a widened horizon, which changes the whole thinking and it feels great.

I easily pay the monthly costs for maintaining a larger apartment.

B: I buy higher quality foods. My health benefits from better food and it makes me feel much better.

C: It is fun to entertain friends. The dining table can easily be enlarged and the living room can accommodate quite a few people. I usually have a party service. They bring and cook the food and clean up afterwards.

D: The best of it all is the indoor swimming pool. It makes an incredible difference in my wellbeing. I am swimming first thing in the morning and come energized to work, and late afternoon, right after I finish my workday.

E: In August I pan a vacation to …. (fill in where you want to go).

When you have a large goal, if possible divide it into tinier goals.

If you want to live in a mansion with some land, wish first for an apartment, which is larger as the one in which you live now. Then wish for a house and then for the mansion. Think that you need time to get used to any change, so also for a better lIfestyle.

If you want to earn $/€ 10.000 a month or more, what will you do to earn more money? It does not matter with what kind of work you start making more money. With the time you will get ideas or offers to make a lot more money. You have to get active in order to give money a chance getting into your life. If you do not know how to earn more money, start with something, no matter how much or little you earn.

Build up slowly.

I now earn $ 1.500 monthly or more and I am so happy that I will continuously earn more money.

I now earn $ 3.000 monthly or more and I am so happy that I will continuously earn more money.

I now earn $ 5.000 monthly or more and I am so happy that I will continuously earn more money.

I now earn $ 10.000 monthly or more and I am so happy that I will continuously earn more money.

I now earn $ 20.000 monthly or more and I am so happy that I will continuously earn more money.

I now earn $ 50.000 monthly or more and I am so happy that I will continuously earn more money.

Answer the questions for each stage of your increased income:

What will you do with the money? How will your life change? How will you feel?

While you do this, you have to think about what is important to you in the next step after you reached your next money goal. Do it in writing. You will appreciate thinking about what else you will be able to afford with each step.

"It is a good feeling to know that I make my dreams come true. I know that I will reach the next step of my financial goal. I now earn $ xx.000 a month and I am continuously earning more money."

Note: When you read this sentence once or twice a day and visualize your life after you have reached your next money goal and nothing happens in your life or your income goes up and down, be patient. There are blocks which you have to pass.

Let us write another script

I get up in the morning filled with energy and I am looking forward to a great and productive day.

First thing in the morning I am swimming, which is so refreshing and it makes me feel great.

For breakfast I have fresh fruit and then eggs sunny side up.

I am in a wonderful mood when I start working. I am really passionate about my work. I get all done in time, which I have planned for the day.

I start my after-working hours working out in my home gym.

My Mercedes drives smoothly. It feels like sitting in a living room with view.

I take time for a nutritious dinner. It is the time when the family is together and sometimes I entertain friends. I really appreciate this time

After going to bed I read a book. Before falling asleep I think back to a great day and am looking forward to another wonderful day, which will be filled with productive work and a lot of joy.

I am really happy about my life.

Note: Whatever you wish in your next step, put feelings to it also in writing. "I enjoy, I have fun, I really like, it feels great…."

Do not make your script too long. I recommend that you read it in the morning and in the evening, which is easy when it is not longer as one page. Reading your script twice a day is also a repetition in addition to your visualizations and helps programming your system (subconscious mind).

Your perception will change and so will your lifestyle. It will change in a way you can't imagine today. With the time you will have new wishes and you will adjust your script making additions and changes.

Always think how important your thoughts are and how you feel. Your thoughts and emotions are the building blocks of your future.

Chapter 35: Meditation And Visualization

Meditation and visualization are both enabling tools that can help improve your consciousness and self-awareness. They are also very useful in helping your mind to focus. Visualization is a good way to bring positive energies to your body, mind and spirit and to expand your creativity.

Visualization In Meditation

When you meditate, you allow your mind to focus while your body relaxes. This is basically the same position you can use for effective visualization. You can opt to read a visualization or relaxation script during your session but you are always free to create your own. When your mind is focused and your body is free from stress and tension, you can start engaging your imagination to visualize concepts and images. You can use both visualization and meditation to teach you and heal you.

Allow the visualization process to help you control your body through your mind.

If you want to begin incorporating visualization in your meditation sessions, you can use this simple relaxation script: "Inhaling, I relax. Exhaling, I smile". Recite this mantra over and over as many times as you want. As you do so, visualize how your body relaxes with every breath.

Benefits of Visualization

Research studies show that visualization can bring a lot of notable benefits to the physical body such as improved immune system, relieved depression, headaches, chronic pains and insomnia and reduced stress. If you want to practice meditation and visualization for better health, you need to practice them on a daily basis to build stronger connections between your mind and body. You can find several visualization scripts (both in audio and video) to guide your practice. Just always remember not to be attached to the outcome of your practice. Instead, focus on your journey towards recovery.

Basic Steps for Visualization

1.   Completely clear your mind of all distractions. You can do this by focusing on your own breath.

2.   Create an idea or picture in your head before you start the session. It is ideal to choose general ideas like joy, love or positive affirmations ("I am balanced").

3.   As you breathe in, feel how your body expands with potential. As you breathe out, release your positive thoughts out to the world.

Chapter 36: Get 100 Percent Focused

And Become Limitless!

Think of focus as an ability that you have to fight for. It is not something that comes naturally or you can switch on and off at will. Now that you have learned the different techniques on how to improve your focus, you can now come up with your own unique formula on how to practice it every day. This final chapter will help you put it all together.

Change your mind set. As cliché as this might sound, when you truly believe that you will be focused, you will. Every day, tell yourself that you are a focused person and eventually your actions will follow your words. Every day, practice the visualization, NLP and meditation techniques that will help you develop this mindset.

Use pen and paper. The first step is to make use of offline tools to organize your thoughts. Using gadgets can tempt you into going online and getting distracted for hours, literally! Think of your gadget as a tool, and your pen and paper as another set of tools so that you will appreciate using both instead of relying too much on apps.

Create a "focus" card. This is a simple piece of paper or card on which you write down what you need to focus on today. Keep this card with you all throughout the day and make sure that you can see it while you are working.

Break down big tasks. A major project will seem too difficult, but if you break it down to smaller, more manageable tasks you will be able to focus better without feeling overwhelmed. As soon as you have set a goal, grab a pen and paper and create a step by step process on how to achieve that goal. Make it as detailed as possible and include the time and date of when you would like to accomplish them. Create deadlines and remind yourself of them so that you will think twice before letting yourself get distracted.

Identify your Laziness Pattern. We all have bouts of laziness throughout our day. Start monitoring how you spend your own day so that you will know when you are starting to feel lazy and plan your breaks around those times. Likewise, determine the times of the day when you feel powered up and fully focused. You can plan on working during those times as well.

Set time limits. Deadlines are a great motivating factor to keep you focused.

When in doubt, unplug. Remember that you do not want to encourage multitasking if your goal is to maximize your focus. Therefore it will be counterproductive for you if you have multiple devices turned on and you are working in an environment full of distractions if your one goal is, say, to study for an exam. Once you have decided upon a goal and a process on how to achieve it, unplug everything else that is not related to the task. That way, your chances of getting distracted will dramatically decrease.

Keep a productivity journal. To help monitor your productivity for the day, make it a habit to answer this short question in your journal before you turn in for the night, "What were the productive tasks that I was able to do today?" Reflecting on how well you spent your day will encourage you to continue developing your good habits, while looking at where you went wrong will help you make the necessary adjustments.

Impose focus. When it all boils down to it, you have the opportunity to choose between letting yourself get distracted or staying focused. There will be times within the day when you are tempted to peek at your phone, open up the browser and check your email, or go out with your friends instead of focusing on the important task at hand. Whenever you face this situation, say out loud, "I am too focused to get distracted" or come up with your own declarative statement to keep you from straying.

Conclusion

I hope you like this book. If you liked the book; kindly review the book.

About The Author

Andrew Maltz is born wth the vision to promote the art of Visualization among the masses. The author has written several research papers on the topic. He has served as an instructor promoting various cultural arts in University of San Francisco. He is currently living with his wife in Toronto.

CPSIA information can be obtained
at www.ICGtesting.com
Printed in the USA
LVHW080952020623
748733LV00012B/178